The Creatively Gifted Child

THE CREATIVELY GIFTED CHILD

SUGGESTIONS FOR PARENTS AND TEACHERS

by Joe Khatena

VANTAGE PRESS
New York Washington Atlanta Hollywood

FIRST EDITION

All rights reserved, including the right of
reproduction in whole or in part in any form.

Copyright © 1978 by Joe Khatena

Published by Vantage Press, Inc.
516 West 34th Street, New York, New York 10001

Manufactured in the United States of America
Standard Book Number 533-03240-7

DEDICATION

I dedicate this book to my wife Nelly, my children Annette, Allan, Moshe and Serena, and my friends and teachers John Gowan and Paul Torrance without whom it would never have happened.

ACKNOWLEDGMENTS

I acknowledge the generosity of the author John C. Gowan and the publishers Personnel Press, the *Gifted Child Quarterly*, and the *Journal of Creative Behavior* for granting me permission to quote their published works. In addition I also thank the various authors and publishers whose writings have been quoted in brief under the "fair use" rule. Further I am grateful to both E. Paul Torrance and John C. Gowan for reading the entire manuscript and for making helpful suggestions to enhance the book. I owe so much to so many for shaping my thoughts on the subject of the book and in particular my wife and children who taught me to understand better the creatively gifted child.

CONTENTS

Foreword by E. Paul Torrance

Introduction by Dr. John C. Gowan

1: Familiar Tales   1
   Ike   1
   Mary   3
   Jim   4
   John   5
   Teacher Power   7
   Parent Power   9
   Some Thoughts to Share   10
2: Changing Concepts of Intelligence   13
   Binet and Intelligence   14
   Stanford Binet   15
   Wechsler and Intelligence   15
   Intelligence as Many Abilities   15
   Intelligence Measures Predicting School Achievement   16
   Some Measures of Intelligence and Achievement   16
   Structure of Intellect Model   17
   Intelligence and Creativity   20
3: Some Measures of Creative Thinking Abilities   23
   A Few Definitions of Creativity   23
   Four Creative Thinking Abilities   24
   Two Approaches to the Measurement of Creativity   28
   Guilford's Creativity Tests for Children   28
   Torrance Tests of Creative Thinking   35
   Thinking Creatively with Sounds and Words   40

    Other Information About the Guilford and Torrance Measures 44
    List of Common, Unoriginal Responses to Demonstrator Form 45
4: An Instrument for Parents and Teachers 49
    Something About Myself 51
    Criteria for Identification, Diagnosis, and Facilitation 53
    A Four-step Plan of Action 53
    Some Clues About Creative Perceptions 54
    An Instance of the Model at Work 56
5: Some Activities to Stimulate Creative Thinking 61
    Stimulating the Creative Imagination 63
    Analogy 71
    Imagery 73
    Figures of Speech as Analogy Forms 74
    Figures of Speech in Analogies 76
    Using Analogy to Solve Problems 80
    Analogy and Creative Writing 82
6: Some Problems of Creatively Gifted Children 85
    Adjustment of Creative Children 87
    Problems of Repressing Creative Needs 89
    Parent and Teacher as Counselor 91
    Some Ways to Prevent These Problems 92
7: Creative Development of the Child 97
    Stages of Creative Development 97
    Development as Continuous 104
    Relationship Between the Two Approaches 106
    Counteracting Measures 106
8: Parent and Teacher Hold the Key 109
References 117

FOREWORD

At birth, some children appear to be far more creative than others. They are active and energetic. They seem to observe everything and respond to every sound, odor, or image. They learn quickly how to communicate their needs and wants and how to interpret the behavior of the people about them. They examine everything and as soon as they can crawl around, they "stick their noses into everything." We say that they are curious.

Strangely, however, these individual differences in creativity that seem to exist at birth are wiped out by the way this curiosity and creative energy are treated by parents and others who play important roles in the lives of young children. As children grow older, individual differences in creativity seem to be the result almost entirely of experience rather than heredity. Since the activity and curiosity of very young children are an inconvenience to adults, these characteristics are discouraged. The more energetic and the more curious a child is, the more likely is he to be punished for such behavior.

These conclusions are not just the speculations of psychologists and educators. They are supported by many studies. Perhaps the most compelling evidence comes from studies of identical and fraternal twins. This has been the psychologist's favorite way of determining the heritability of various characteristics. In fact, psychologists such as Cyril Burt in England and Arthur Jensen in California have compared identical twins with fraternal twins to establish most of their claims for the heritability of intelligence. In these studies they have shown that identical twins are more similar in intelligence to one another than are fraternal twins.

Psychologists are finding now that identical twins are no more like one another than fraternal twins in creative abilities. Let's look at the results of some of these twin studies.

Bert O. Richmond, one of my colleagues at the University of Georgia, studied five pairs of fraternal twins and eight pairs of identical twins. All of them were administered the *Torrance Tests of Creative Thinking*, both those requiring verbal responses and those requiring figural responses (drawing). On none of these performances was there evidence of heritability. The identical twins were just as different from one another as the fraternal twins.

Thomas R. Pezzullo of the University of Rhode Island and Eric E. Thorsen and George F. Madaus of Boston College conducted a similar study of 28 pairs of identical twins and 37 pairs of fraternal twins in Massachusetts. In addition to some of the activities of the *Torrance Tests of Creative Thinking*, they administered these pairs of twins tests similar to those used by Jensen in his studies of the heritability of intelligence. One set of these tests might be called measures of "general intelligence" and the other would be considered tests of short-term memory. While these researchers found strong evidence for the heritability of general intelligence and moderate evidence for the heritability of short-term memory, they found no evidence for the heritability of such creative thinking abilities as figural and verbal fluency, flexibility, and originality. In other words, the pairs of identical twins were no more similar to one another in creativity than the pairs of fraternal twins.

All of these facts make extremely important the things that Joe Khatena says in this book. If creative behavior were determined by heredity, there would be little that parents could do to increase it. There is compelling evidence that this is not true. How a young child's creative behavior is treated by parents and other important people in his life seems to make "all of the difference."

In this book, Joe Khatena speaks with considerable authority. A considerable part of his professional career has been devoted to efforts to understand and facilitate the development of the creative abilities of children and adults. He has developed a number of tests of creative abilities and personality characteristics and has developed instructional materials for teaching both young children and adults to think more creatively. He is also the father of four highly creative children, so he also writes from his rich personal experience as a father as well as from his experiences in helping other parents of highly creative children.

For almost 20 years, I have been hoping that someone would write a book like this. I am very proud that Dr. Joe Khatena, one of my former students, has accomplished this pioneering feat.

E. Paul Torrance
Department of Educational Psychology
The University of Georgia
Athens, Georgia 30602
September 9, 1977

INTRODUCTION

It is a double pleasure to write an introduction for a former student who has succeeded in accomplishing a task not satisfactorily handled before. For Professor Khatena has written the first authoritative and competent book for parents of gifted children. It not only directs parents and teachers to the principal importance of giftedness, namely its potentiality for verbal creativity, but it also represents at the same time a tract popular enough to be read by the layman, yet possessed of the research background which has resulted in Professor Khatena's presidency of the National Association for Gifted Children.

Other more amateur authors have attempted the same task, but they have tended to celebrate the giftedness of the child as if that were the accomplishment instead of the promise. We would never make such a mistake in athletics, for potential there is only something to be developed into performance. Further, we do not consider it undemocratic or unethical for football players to have a special coach who requires special practice and training, enforces segregation of an elect few, and who would be fired immediately if he let everyone who wanted to play in the big game do so. Football and other professional sports are important in our culture. Creativity it appears is not.

But there comes a time (as Toynbee foretold) in every culture when the creative minority has become the dominant minority and can no longer respond successfully to the challenges of the environment. When that happens, a series of recurrent crises results, an internal proletariat (in but not of the culture) develops in the cities and barbarian war bands prey on the culture from outside. How prescient! The only solution in Toynbee's view is to find new creative responses to cultural challenges. Where can such responses be found?

Eight thousand years ago Man made such a creative response. He discovered agriculture—that is the domestication of animals and vegetables so that he did not have to hunt for his food as a nomad. History and civilization were born out of that domestication.

Today, we are in a similar fix. For we gather creativity wild, that is, we use as creative only those few eccentrics out of whom the family, the church, education, government and business cannot extirpate. Naturally such individuals tend to be antisocial types. Suppose we were to cultivate and domesticate creativity—to reward it in our homes and schools; to develop it to the fullest—we would see a renaissance the like of which would make Periclean Athens the golden age of Rome, the *Risorgemento* in Italy and all the rest seem sterile. For such rare periods in history are simply the accidental coming together of a small creative minority but with a "critical mass" to liberate more energy than they dissipate. We can have such a culture and the society we have may be our own. Dr. Khatena tells you how to start it in your home today.

Dr. John C. Gowan, editor of the *Gifted Child Quarterly*
& Executive Director — National Asociation
for Gifted Children

The Creatively Gifted Child

1: Familiar Tales

Parents and teachers often do not find it easy to talk about children who are gifted especially if the children are their own. Some gifted children use their talents in a productive way and may be referred to as *creatively gifted*. In trying to be themselves, to learn, to do things, to make friends, and to get to know their world better, creatively gifted children may experience considerable difficulty. More often than not people do not recognize or understand them. Often they get into situations that obstruct them from doing the things in the way best suited to their healthy growth, and that place them in conflict with others, with consequent problems. As a result when parents and teachers are asked to choose between gifted children who are creative and those who are not, they usually choose those who are not creative, since these children nearly always are less troublesome both at home and in school.

IKE

A few days ago J. J. called me from a nearby town in Kentucky to tell me about his seven-year-old son Ike: "To be sure he is a smart boy, but how smart I do not know except that Ike does and says things in a special way. I wonder if you know anyone who can tell me more about my boy, how bright he is, and what help he can get to learn as a bright boy should."

That same weekend I saw J. J. at a workshop. He was chosen from the audience to participate in an activity on the raised platform of the auditorium with seven others. They were asked to imagine they were eggs in a carton just put in a refrigerator. A number of questions followed, which were designed to heighten their sensitivity and prepare them for creative thinking. To the question, "As an egg, how would you like to be used?" J. J. spontaneously replied, "To make swine-flu vaccine."

A week later he brought Ike to my office as had been pre-arranged. "So you are the man who liked Mrs. Smith's blueberry pie," commented Ike as soon as we were introduced. We settled down and Ike began to draw pictures once I started him on *Thinking Creatively With Pictures*, a measure devised by Torrance (1974) to find out how creative a person is without having to use words. Ike finished his first picture in just four minutes with six minutes to spare, and was ready for the next task. He said he had nothing more to add to it and had given it a title as well. While Ike was busy doing other pictures, J. J. and his wife told me that Ike had questioned them about seeing me. After being told that he had been specially chosen for a study I was doing he said, "Then I will be a mouse." That was what Ike had drawn as his first picture.

Later in the week J. J. and his wife visited me, and I showed them what Ike had drawn, and what the pictures told us about him. They observed that Ike had drawn all the pictures required, and some very interesting and different kinds of pictures. Soon we were talking about how fluent Ike was, as shown by the many pictures he had drawn. His flexible thinking became apparent by the many different kinds of objects he had included. He had also drawn some very unusual and clever pictures, which told us that his ability to think originally was high. One thing he did not seem to want to do was to add many details to the "mouse" drawing. I recalled that when he had completed all the essential details of the mouse, he considered the picture done. Ike scored very high on fluency, flexibility, originality, and elaboration—the four terms used by Torrance to describe the creative thinking abilities of a person. Ike, we would say, is a highly creative boy.

J. J. and his wife went away understanding something about Ike's potential gifts. Although they recognized that the school Ike attended did not do much to develop his creative thinking abilities, they were convinced that something could be done for him and for others like him. They then decided to read a book I had suggested to learn some of the things they could do to help Ike at home and to begin drawing together parents who felt as they did so as to organize a group to help them better understand their children's creative potential and assist their children in developing these abilities. Further, they said that they would talk to Ike's teacher and get her on their side to help Ike in school.

MARY

Mary was regarded by all her teachers as an excellent student. She did her work on time, scored the highest grades in her class, and got along well with schoolmates. A psychologist on the Board of Education said she was exceptionally bright, and tests showed her to have an I.Q. of 158. Her dad and I shared a pizza one day a few years ago, and we talked of Mary as the smartest person in his family, who had no opportunity in school for quicker and fuller growth of her intellectual talents. He had heard that I had helped others find out if their children were creative and wondered if I would do the same for Mary.

Soon afterwards, Mary was in my office taking the *Torrance Tests of Creative Thinking With Words and Pictures*. She was well mannered, listened to instructions with care, and did the tests that were given to her. Her scores indicated that she was quite average on all four creative thinking abilities, namely, fluency, flexibility, originality, and elaboration, although she scored higher on the test with words. Her father was disappointed although I had forewarned him that it was not unusual for children with high I. Q. to be average or above average in creative thinking abilities. Three years passed before Mary was included in a newly begun program for gifted children. She is still one of the brightest in her school, is president of the Honors Society, makes straight A's, and will no doubt be ready for early admission to college.

JIM

Just last week I had a call from a distressed parent, who was my wife's fellow college student, about her nine-year-old son. They lived in Ohio, and Jim was with her away from school for the day. That same afternoon they visited me, and I observed that he was very bright but did not do his school work well or achieve high grades consistently. He was a pain in the neck to some of his teachers, preferred to learn things on his own, knew quite a lot about many things in the encyclopedia, had invented a more efficient clothes rack, and had just designed a system of pulleys to help his mother, who had a back condition, walk up two flights of stairs.

I screened Jim and found him to be very bright. His I. Q. was 140, and he was highly creative as well. Jim was having trouble with his school work not because of lack of ability, but as I found out later, because he was not challenged by schooling, was generally bored, and was very much distressed by his peers whenever he obtained high grades. The problem was accentuated by the fact that no special educational provisions exist in their state, which might have helped Jim overcome some of his difficulties and do what he was really capable of doing.

Next is John, a creatively gifted person, who obviously was not understood by his teachers, who was miserable as a student, and who by sheer energy of his creative potential survived it all to become a person of high achievement in spite of the system. It may be that if his teachers had been sensitive to his needs and recognized him as someone special, he would not have been miserable. Wise channelling of the boy's high creative potential would have led to productivity of excellence and greater fulfillment in the life of the child with resultant benefits to his community.

JOHN

John is a very dear friend, and just the other day while we were talking about our children and children of other families, John mellowed into reminiscence about himself:

"Like a billion others I was shaped by formal schooling. When I was little I remember my mother dressing me for school. I entered into grade one and sweated it out for twelve years.

"I used to dream quite a lot even at seven, and this annoyed my teachers. I often found myself wearing a dunce cap or a basket—not that I minded the ignoble costume, but to have to face the rest with eyes peeping sheepishly through that intricately woven contraption was upsetting in no small way. I was convinced my teacher did not understand me, but that was not unusual because I didn't understand myself. I was easily bored and punished for being naughty. The years slipped by and so did I—from one grade to the next.

"Once a week I had to sing as the other boys. I tried to tell my teacher it wouldn't work but at the point of her piercing eyes I croaked in a voice better silent the lovely lines, 'All things bright and beautiful . . .' At thirteen I tried not to be heard, and by fourteen definitely hated music. However, I found myself a professional musician at sixteen and loving every bit of it.

"The only lesson I really liked in school was Spoken English, and that was because we had a teacher of vitality with a booming voice, a kindly gentleman who spoke faultlessly except for an occasional 'umph!' a deep breath, and the inevitable boom. But I loved him and the familiar crunch of boot on gravel. The entry made, the furniture moved, and we along with it. Then followed an hour of pure delight in the drama of the court house, the marketplace, the nobleman's castle enacting scenes of real life and fantasy.

"Of course I disliked grade eight history. I had a teacher whose target was the chair, with foot thrust in bottom drawer of desk, a subtle clicking of the tongue and smooth oscillation of the head in quick survey of forty cringing devils. 'Turn to Chapter 3 . . . and read the next eleven pages.' Sixteen minutes later, a thump or two delivered with precision on two or three backs hunched in pretended industry, and we knew at once the prowler was at large again. A week before the exams, a fog of chalk dust emerged from the green board, and with tired inky fingers we were painfully scratching the forty-ninth page of notes. It took me the better part of ten years to get rid of that gritty historical chalk dust to major in college history.

"I almost learned mathematics in school. But mathematical relations were slapped into me. For instance, one teacher who taught me geometry thought that proximity to him and the figural representation of two isosceles triangles would aid my understanding of their relationship. He made significant feet movements as he manipulated his palm, and I like many others learned to anticipate a right slap when the left foot was raised. I saw, ducked, and felt the impact of both hands on my face. Pythagoras must have squirmed!

"The geography teacher was in contrast good, but between church and scouting activities I had little of him or geography.

"Oddly enough it was not until I was 35 years old that I found myself, and why I behaved the way I did. I never could do as well as my classmates when it came to remembering facts and repeating them when called upon to do so in the many examinations our teachers devised for us—of course this did not mean that I could not remember those things I wanted to remember! But when it came to writing of a dramatic sequence or story, I did quite as well if not better than most of my classmates. But then we were not asked to use our imagination too much in school; we were being prepared for the real hard facts of life!

"I became interested in poetry a few years after high school. Somehow I never really enjoyed poetry lessons. I guess because my teachers were too concerned with giving lessons and missed the whole point about poetic experience and its appeal to the intellect, emotion, and imagination. We learned lines by heart but forgot them even quicker. Recitation was for the most part boring and painful, and somehow quite embarrassing to me as I crunched my way through the stony path of words.

"When I played the guitar, I enjoyed ad-lib more than I did the tune itself. Somehow the school had inhibited the development of my talents. I noticed this even more when at the age of twenty-six, I began writing many poems some of which have since been published.

"Stage make up excited me quite a bit and what I enjoyed most was to create faces for fantasy characters like Caliban or do unusual and difficult character make up requiring the use of invention.

"Now that I look back I realize the poverty of my school experience in the realm of the imagination. If only my teachers had been sensitive enough to spot me out as a dreamer or troubled to provide experiences that were rich, stimulating, and challenging both to the intellect and imagination, my heartaches, wasted energies and time could have been prevented."

TEACHER POWER

The day before a meeting of the National Association for Gifted Children I met a couple, parents interested in their gifted nine-year-old son who was reading at the twelfth grade level. They expressed concern that the child came home from school with books suitable for a third grader because there were no advanced level books in the class to read. Since the teacher gave points for the number of books read regardless of their quality in terms of reading age, the boy would take home scrimpy little books. In this way he could claim having read a great number of books.

We as teachers should certainly be on our guard for such discrepancy, anticipate reading deception, and provide challenging reading experiences for such children. Children with extraordinary ability or talent often become bored with regular schooling. Although there have been many attempts by both educational agencies and highly sensitive teachers to provide enrichment to the public school curriculum, the programs are still geared to the average student and not the creatively gifted. Perhaps you as the class teacher, more than anyone else in that setting, are privileged to deal with the problem. You are in a face-to-face situation with the needs of your creative students and their exceptional talent, and this can certainly be the start of many wonderful things for such students and a great adventure for you as well. You can enhance your students' development in so many different ways so as to stir them to think productively, to arouse their curiosity, to excite their imagination, and to help them look at the world as a place where wonderful discoveries await. You can do these things by arranging circumstances in the classroom and acting as catalyst for their creative interaction with the world. Flexibility, improvisation, and invention should be your constant companions. If you give the creative student half the chance he will come to you for counsel and confide in you from time to time. So be prepared for this as he will need you.

PARENT POWER

Recently a parent wrote to the Editor of the *Gifted Child Quarterly*, a journal produced by the National Association for Gifted Children, expressing her concern for her child, who she knew was gifted, and the impact she anticipated this would have on others in her community if she were to talk about it:

> If I were to say that I had a retarded or physically handicapped child, people would believe me. No one would resent me, and most reactions would be sympathetic. Having a gifted child, however, I know I do better keeping quiet. People wouldn't believe me. 'Another bragging mother,' I would be called ... In a small town, especially, it is wiser not to mention it (Oppen, 1970, p. 92).

This mother is not alone in her perception of the complications of having the gifted child recognized in the community. Instead of finding increased joy in sharing what really is a community resource she feels the need to hide it from others for fear of being scorned, envied, and even hurt. She is not necessarily responsible for her ignorance since she like so many others is the product of cultural processing.

I would like to suggest to you that as parents of the creatively gifted child, you are the most significant people in the child's life and by far the most potent lead to the child's attempts to realize his or her full potential. Thus it is so important that you understand your creatively gifted child and have the right kind of attitudes toward him or her.

McCall's Magazine carried the story entitled "Living With People" at one time, in which is described the relationship of Gail Sheehy and her daughter whose team work led to the writing of their novel *Love-Sounds*.

Recall the true story reported several years ago on the "Today Show" of an Irish novelist who as a child wrote a

novel of great strength using his toe (taking twelve years to complete since the rest of him was paralyzed). He did so because his mother showed him love and understanding, made him feel significant, gave meaning to his life, and showed great appreciation for his talent. The mother had done for the Irish novelist at home what Plato had advocated the state should do for the young when he stated that "What is honored in one's own country is what will be cultivated." I am sure that is what most of us would like to do for our creatively gifted children if we could.

SOME THOUGHTS TO SHARE

These are not unusual stories of gifted children and their parents and teachers. The stories tell us about the concerns and difficulties parents experience with gifted children when trying to decide how they can help their children achieve the best in this world. Certainly they are concerned about understanding their children better, knowing how bright their children are, and what they can do to select the best schooling for them.

Children can have a hard time in school and not really understand why. Some of us notice that a child in the family is unusually bright just by what he says and does (often this is a very helpful way of knowing that we have someone special with us). Others among us, although we care for our children and do observe them during work and play, do not know what to look for. When we do become aware that we have someone worthy of special attention, we do not really know that there are some things we as parents and teachers can do for them. If we are able to spot gifted children early enough, then we can begin to understand why some become easily bored or impatient, why some rebel and get into trouble, and why some after a time do not seem to care and sacrifice their talents to become like everyone else.

We as parents and teachers have become overly dependent on outside sources for help when we have access to so many of our own at home or in the classroom. To find out how bright our children are, we as parents often hope or wait for the teacher to tell us either face-to-face or by test grades and report cards. Sometimes the information is adequate and sometimes it is not. Often we depend too heavily upon the psychologist for clues about the talent of our children. Obviously we should not administer or evaluate psychological tests since they are designed by them for their use, and to do so we would need special training. And of course this is not to say that we do not need the help of both teacher and psychologist; we most certainly do. But we do not want to be like over-anxious parents who rush their children to the doctor for the most trivial reason.

There are some things we can do at home or in the classroom both to identify our children with special abilities and to help them grow more healthily by encouraging them to use their gifts and talents productively. What we can do as parents and teachers may be of very special advantage to all concerned especially when neither outside help nor unique schooling opportunity is available. Of course the time may come when our children will have to compete with other children for placement in special programs for the talented and gifted, at which time our children will stand a better chance to be selected for these programs, and we will have to have our children more formally screened. In any case the advantages will be great for both our gifted children and ourselves. We will certainly have more experiences to draw us closer together; our sensitivity to their growth towards fulfillment as they struggle to get command of their world would be increased, and our awareness of their problems and the way we can help them overcome them become heightened.

I know that as parents and teachers our task is as difficult as it is rewarding, but the privilege is ours to unlock the potential of the gifted to its fullest realization. Socrates once said "the teacher is not one who crams the minds of the students with the greatest number of facts in the shortest time, but the one who is able to kindle a fire of spiritual and intellectual enthusiasm; who develops within the student a knowledge of what he can become." As this is relevant to the teacher so is it significant for the parent who assumes the role of teacher as well.

2: Changing Concepts of Intelligence

We still do not know everything about identifying the gifted child although we know a lot more about it today than we did seventy years ago. It is one thing to decide what qualities and behaviors qualify a human being to be called gifted, and another to be able to successfully measure them so that we may find out if one person is more or less gifted than another.

It took most of us about half a century to realize that a person may be gifted in many different ways. The first most productive theory was that of general intelligence, which later found expression in the term I.Q. or Intelligence Quotient. It was found that, if we knew a person's I.Q., we could quite safely predict how well he could do in school. As we obtained more information on I.Q. we came to understand that one person may be able to demonstrate his intelligence without using words whereas another person may do so using words.

An important breakthrough came when we realized that in trying to identify intelligence and give it a number value like I.Q., we were not talking of raw intelligence but of potential expressed through experience about the world gained with and without the use of words. So it was decided that intellect would be a better term to use. Consequently, earlier thoughts about intelligence have taken on a new dimension in the concept of intelligence as a center for processing information received and given out. The Structure of Intellect, as it was called, in addition to the processing capabilities of the earlier theories of intelligence, namely, knowing, remembering, reasoning that leads to one right answer, and judging, had a fifth processing ability involving reasoning that leads to many possible solutions to a problem, namely, divergent thinking, which also has been described as creative thinking.

BINET AND INTELLIGENCE

In the early years of this century a Frenchman, Alfred Binet, was given the task of finding some way to identify those children who could benefit from schooling and those who could not. His search led him to construct an instrument that was meant to tell us how well a child could understand, reason, and judge, how adaptable and persistent he could be, and the extent to which he could apply self-criticism. Binet thought of all these mental abilities as general intelligence. He had the brilliant idea that if a child could perform the activities related to these ways of thinking the same as other children his own age, he possessed average intelligence. Thus if he were five years old and could do the tests that other five-year-old children could do, he would have a mental age or M.A. of five years. Of course if a five-year-old child could do the activities of a seven- or eight-year-old child, then he would be considered highly gifted. Later two psychologists expanded Binet's concept to Intelligence Quotient or for short I.Q. The child who was 5 years old and had a mental age of 7 would have an I.Q. of 140. One of these men who taught us how to derive an I.Q. was Lewis Terman, a professor at Stanford University. He made Binet's test suitable for use in America and called it *Stanford Binet* after his university.

STANFORD BINET

The *Stanford Binet* was found to be very helpful since it could tell us that if a child obtained a high I.Q. he stood a very good chance of doing well in his schooling, and if a child obtained a low I.Q. he would very likely need special learning opportunities. The *Stanford Binet* became a very useful diagnostic tool; that is to say it can be used to pick out strengths and weaknesses in the mental functioning of the child, giving clues about his mental health that may determine what can be done to help him. As a result it has been used widely by psychologists in clinics and hospitals.

WECHSLER AND INTELLIGENCE

Another American psychologist, David Wechsler, has measures of intelligence for children and adults producing an I.Q. that evaluates a person when words do not have to be used, and a combined I.Q. that aims at telling how bright a person is in general. Wechsler has defined intelligence as "the aggregate or global capacity of the individual to act purposefully, to think rationally and to deal effectively with his environment." (Wechsler, 1966, p. 7.)

INTELLIGENCE AS MANY ABILITIES

Several other American psychologists have added to our understanding of intelligence. From them we have learned that a person can be intelligent in many different ways. L. L. Thurstone, for instance, told us that there is little or no relationship between the many ways we can be bright and an overall brightness that is equated with general intelligence. He explained that the most important of these abilities are: verbal comprehension or understanding when words are used; word fluency or using words easily in speaking and writing; handling spatial relations or relations of things that can be seen, touched, or heard; working with numbers; reasoning or thinking in a logical way; and seeing relations among patterns or perceptual relations.

INTELLIGENCE MEASURES PREDICTING SCHOOL ACHIEVEMENT

As I have mentioned earlier, Binet constructed his measure of general intelligence with the purpose of identifying which children could benefit from schooling and which could not. Over the years we have found that children identified as bright by the *Stanford Binet* achieved well in school and obtained high grades, and those who were identified as unable to benefit from regular schooling did not learn well and obtained very low grades in school. So we became convinced that I.Q. and achievement were highly related. In other words by knowing someone's I.Q. we could predict how successful he would be in school. Sometimes we could use achievement tests to find out how well a person will do or is doing in school directly, since the evidence we have does suggest that high achievers are most often highly intelligent people.

SOME MEASURES OF INTELLIGENCE AND ACHIEVEMENT

Until the 1950s, we could measure a child's capacity to learn by using measures like the *Stanford Binet* or the *Wechsler Scales of Intelligence*, which are individual tests given by trained testers, or by using group tests that are supposed to measure a similar kind of mental capacity like the *California Test of Mental Maturity*, the *Raven's Progressive Matrices*, and the *Goodenough Draw-a-Man Test*. An individual test is administered to one person at a time. In addition, tests that measure many mental abilities were also used, such as the *Primary Mental Abilities Tests*, *Differential Aptitude Test*, and the *Multiple Aptitude Test*. To these may be added measures of achievement like the *Stanford Achievement Test*, *California Achievement*, and the *Metropoliton Test*. This is not to say that these measures are not in use today.

STRUCTURE OF INTELLECT MODEL

However, since Binet, work has been going on to find out even more about intelligence and how we might measure it. After 1950 we became more convinced that we should think of intelligence as a combination of many dimensions of abilities. This has made us realize even more that a person could be gifted in many ways, and that the measures we use should tell us more about these different abilities than just a person's I.Q.

About 26 years ago the well-known American psychologist J. P. Guilford told us that there are 120 different aspects of intelligence even though we do not have tests to measure all of them as yet. To help us understand this concept he pictured these abilities as a cube model with each of the three faces marked to show the different jobs that are done by the intellect as it works on information that reaches the person, and as he gives out information (Guilford, 1967).

Operations

Guilford's model tells us that people may use their intellect in a number of different ways to process raw materials of information. This involves knowing or understanding items of information (cognition), storing or fixing of information in the brain (memory), pulling out this information from storage in the brain to help find a single answer to a problem (convergent thinking) or many possible answers to a problem (divergent thinking), and comparing and judging the worth or value of the information received or produced (evaluation).

Contents

A second face of the intellect model deals with four kinds of information that are handled by the five mental operations just described, namely, figural content, symbolic content, semantic content, and behavioral content. *Figural* content deals with things that can be seen, heard, or touched or recalled as images or mental pictures. *Symbolic* content deals with information in the form of signs or letters that have no meaning in themselves. *Semantic* content deals with information that is meaningful and may appear as pictures or words.

CONTENT
Figural
Symbolic
Semantic
Behavioral

PRODUCTS
Units
Classes
Relations
Systems
Transformation
Implications

OPERATIONS
Evaluation
Divergent Production
Convergent Production
Memory
Cognition

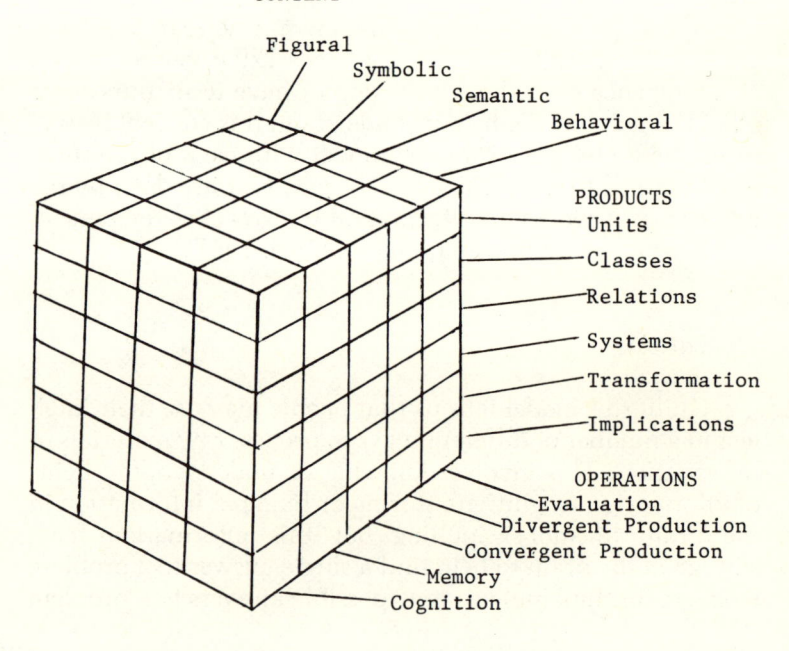

Behavioral content deals with nonverbal information involving attitudes, needs, desires, moods, intentions, and so on that occur when people are interacting with each another.

Products

The third aspect of intellect deals with the different forms information may take when a person processes it. In brief, *units* are things taken as wholes and without analysis like the nouns chair, orange, child, and so on. By combining them in various ways we obtain the remaining five product forms. *Classes* are three or more units of information categorized or grouped together by virtue of their common properties. For instance, the class for the units orange, apple, and banana is fruit, or the class for the units chair, table, bookcase and cupboard is furniture. A *relation* is a meaningful connection between two things such as "John is married to Mary," or "My house is larger than yours." *Systems* are organized sets of units of information that are complexes of interrelated or interacting parts. For instance, this verbally stated arithmetic problem is a system: "The area of this room is 120 square feet and the length is 12 feet. What is the width?" Or the mathematical equation for the distance all around an oblong room as $P = 2(L + B)$ where P is the perimeter, L the length and W the width. *Transformations* are changes in information or in its functioning and involve redefinition, revisions, or modifications, as for instance, from a verb to noun form like "jumping" (from to jump) or "racing" (from to race). An *implication* is something expected, anticipated, or predicted from known information. For example, the most appropriate answer to the problem of deciding where best to locate a hotdog stand will depend upon how well a person can see the consequences of such a decision.

One thing Guilford did was to focus our attention not only on the many ways a person could be intelligent, but also on thinking that could lead to many different alternatives to find answers to problems and to creative production. These abilities are related to divergent thinking, redefinition and transformation abilities in his model of intellectual abilities, sometimes less precisely called creativity.

INTELLIGENCE AND CREATIVITY

The Structure of Intellect does tell us that a person may be bright in many different ways although it is unlikely for him to be bright in all 120 ways. This fact is important for us to understand since it tells us that although we may have the five processing capabilities (cognition, memory, divergent thinking, convergent thinking, and evaluation), not all of them have been used to their fullest potential. This may be one major reason why children, who are intelligent according to I.Q. tests, are sometimes not found to be highly creative when creative measures are used, like the case of Mary in Chapter One. Often for someone to do well on creativity tests he must also be bright in more than an average way. If a person with a high I.Q. is not found to be highly creative we should not conclude that he does not have creative processing capacity, but that he has not had sufficient opportunities and encouragement to use it. If a person with high creative thinking abilities does not have a high I.Q. you may conclude that, since the I.Q. measure does not give such a person the opportunity to show his high creative processing abilities, he is denied the use of this component of his intellect and is really at a disadvantage. If we are to accept Guilford's model of intellectual abilities, then we must recognize that differentiation of I.Q. and creative thinking abilities is an artificial one created more by the measures used than by a person's potential abilities.

The Structure of Intellect Model helps us to recognize that a person may be gifted in nonverbal ways as well. The goal of psychologists and test makers interested in identifying more fully the dimensions of giftedness may very well be the measurement of many verbal and nonverbal abilities including creativity, using as clues some of the important directions set by Guilford.

3: Some Measures of Creative Thinking Abilities

Over the years many people have been interested in creativity and have attempted to define it only to find that the differences in their definitions can be traced to the various aspects of creativity studied at the time. A person may show himself to be creative by the things he makes, by the kind of person he is or the character traits he shows, by the way he reacts when he is pressured or under stress, and by the way he thinks or processes.

A FEW DEFINITIONS OF CREATIVITY

In terms of process, one person may define creative thinking as thinking by analogy. Another defines it as using initiative to stop thinking in the way to which we have become accustomed and try new ways of thinking, to see relationships among things and produce fresh relationships consciously or unconsciously, and to choose and discriminate from many possibilities in order to synthesize and bind them in original ways. Of course it is important to say what you mean by or operationalize creativity before you try to measure it, and at no other time in the history of measurement have we had so many attempts to operationalize creativity.

The notable definitions that have led to the construction of published measures of creativity are those by J. P. Guilford and E. P. Torrance. Remember we talked about creativity in Guilford's intellect model in terms of divergent thinking, redefinition, and transformation abilities. Torrance defines creativity as "the process of sensing gaps or disturbing missing elements, forming hypotheses concerning them, testing these hypotheses, communicating the results, and possibly modifying and retesting these hypotheses." (Torrance, 1962, p. 16.) I have also attempted to define creativity in terms of originality as "the power of the imagination to break away from perceptual set so as to restructure anew ideas, thoughts, and feelings into novel and associative bonds." (Khatena and Torrance, 1973, p. 28.)

FOUR CREATIVE THINKING ABILITIES

Guilford and Torrance stand out as leaders in the measurement of creative thinking abilities. Their tests of creative thinking in general give major roles to four specific thinking abilities, namely fluency, flexibility, originality, and elaboration.

Fluency is the ability to produce many ideas for a given task. Let us say a person is given the task of thinking of many unusual uses of a brick. He may write down "throw it at someone, use it as a paper weight, use it to hold down a pile of clothes, coat it with chocolate and give it to someone as a birthday cake as a joke, and warm it on a fire to iron a shirt." Five unusual uses for a brick have been given. If 1 point is given for each idea produced, the person would score five points for fluency. Of course if he had produced 20 ideas he would have scored 20 points for fluency. The more ideas a person produces, the higher his fluency ability is.

Flexibility is the ability to produce ideas that show a person's movement from one level of thinking to another, or shifts in thinking relative to a given task. Ideas that do the same job do not show shifts in thinking. For instance, two of the unusual uses of bricks namely, "use it as a paper weight" and "use it to hold down a pile of clothes" are the same. In both cases the brick acts as a weight, and there is no shift in thinking. The remaining three ideas, namely, "throw it at someone, coat it with chocolate and give it to someone as a birthday cake for a joke, and warm it on a fire and iron a shirt" do different jobs and show shifts in thinking or flexibility. If one point is awarded for each shift in thought, of the five ideas produced, there are four shifts in thought yielding a flexibility score of four points.

Originality is the ability to produce ideas that not many people think of or that are unusual, remote, and clever. One widely used method of scoring for originality is the awarding of points for ideas produced by 5 people or less out of 100. Too, the ideas are sometimes scaled from 5 points for very new ideas to 1 point for ideas that have been thought of before. Ideas that more than 5 people out of 100 think of are scored 0. Adding all of the points a person obtains for the ideas produced determines his ability to be original.

Elaboration is the ability to add details to a basic idea produced. Suppose a person is given a number of squares, told to think of ideas that no one else would think of, and instructed to draw pictures using the squares. One idea for the drawing of a picture using a square could be "door," and so a door is drawn and a title given to the picture.

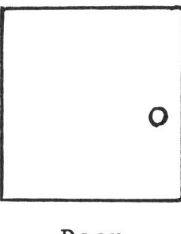

Door

If a person decides to add such details like hinges, decorative structure, extensions to the length, a name plate, a peephole, and so on, he is elaborating on the basic idea of door.

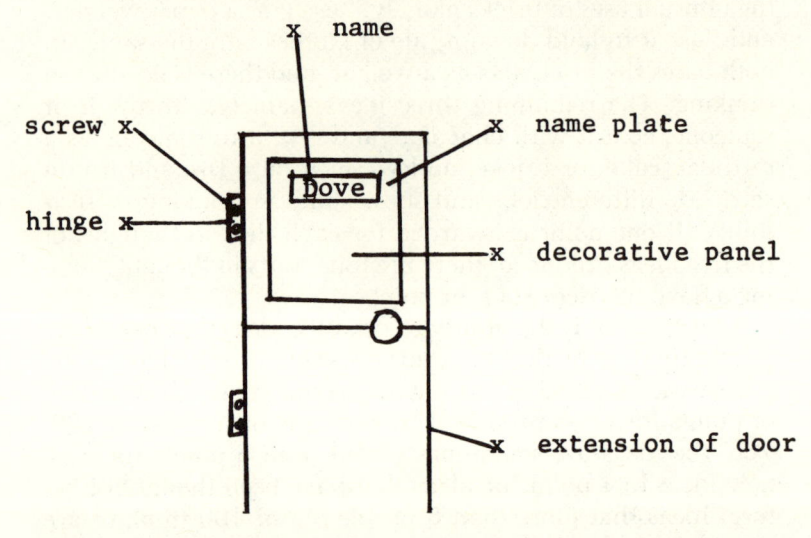

If one point is awarded for every detail added to the basic idea "door," this drawing should fetch an elaboration score of at least seven points. (Each x on the picture indicates one point.) Notice that the doorknob is not scored for elaboration because it is the first detail added to the square to give it the identity of "door." In this way we can determine a person's ability to elaborate.

Common to both Guilford's and Torrance's concepts of creativity and its measurement are fluency, flexibility, originality, and elaboration. However, Guilford tries to measure the four abilities in a way that requires a person to do many test tasks each setting out to give information about 1 of the 24 divergent thinking abilities. On the other hand Torrance tries to measure the same 4 abilities in a way that requires a person to perform several complex tasks each designed to make the person display all of these abilities simultaneously. However, while the Torrance tests identify creative abilities as fluency, flexibility, originality, and elaboration, Guilford's measures use the terms that apply to the Divergent Production Abilities of the Structure of Intellect.

To the four creative thinking abilities (fluency, flexibility, originality, and elaboration) may be added several others recently described by Torrance and his associates (1975) in a streamlined scoring and interpretative manual relative to Figural Form B of the Torrance Tests of Creative Thinking. They are the ability to synthesize and abstract as shown in the production of good titles given to drawings done, Synthesis or the ability to combine two or more figures into a related whole picture, and Closure or the ability to delay completing a task long enough to make the mental leaps that make possible the production of original ideas.

Other dimensions of the creative potential are picked out by reference to the Checklist of Creative Strengths that include the following:

1. Expression of feelings and emotions in the drawings.
2. Articulateness in telling stories with drawings and titles.
3. Movement and action in the drawings (for example, running, dancing, falling, flying, and so on).
4. Expressiveness of titles or labels given to the drawings that communicate feeling or emotion.
5. Combination of two or more incomplete figures (in sequence to make a drawing that shows a process, or in synthesis to produce a new whole).
6. Combination of repeated figures to make a drawing.
7. Unusual visual perspective of an object drawn (for example, viewing it from below, above, or at some unusual angle).
8. Perception of things drawn seen from the inside, underneath, in cross section and so on.
9. Humorous titles or captions given to drawings.
10. Humorous drawings, expressive of figures, positions, combinations, and so on.

11. Drawings that show richness of imagery (variety, vividness, liveliness, and intensity).
12. Drawings that show exciting and unusual imagery.
13. Quickness of warm-up that is seen in the production of original images or drawings early in the sequence of drawings.

TWO APPROACHES TO THE MEASUREMENT OF CREATIVITY

Let us now look at some of the test tasks that Guilford and Torrance designed for children. For our present needs we will look at what Guilford says in *Creativity Tests for Children* (1971), and what Torrance says in his tests *Thinking Creatively with Words and Thinking Creatively with Pictures* (1974), and *Thinking Creatively with Sounds and Words* (Khatena and Torrance, 1973; Torrance, Khatena, and Cunnington, 1973).

GUILFORD'S CREATIVITY TESTS FOR CHILDREN

Guilford's measures of creativity (constructed with help from some of his associates) relate to the Divergent Production Abilities of the Structure or Intellect Model and are meant mainly for children in grades four to six, although he says they can also be used with older children and adults. Generally, the items of the children's tests are revised forms of the adult measures especially in the rewriting of the instructions in a way that children can understand. Only 10 of the 24 Divergent Production Abilities are measured in these tests, and even in the adult forms only measures relating to 18 of the 24 Divergent Production Abilities are described in his book on the *Nature of Human Intelligence* (Guilford, 1967).

Divergent Production Abilities

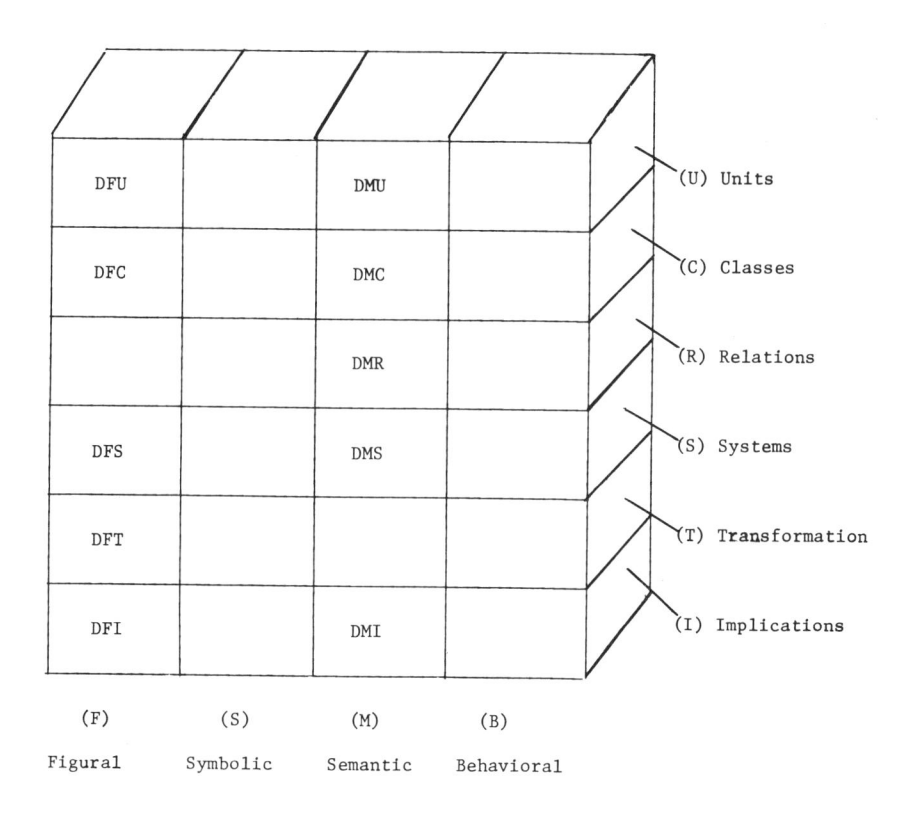

	(F) Figural	(S) Symbolic	(M) Semantic	(B) Behavioral
(U) Units	DFU		DMU	
(C) Classes	DFC		DMC	
(R) Relations			DMR	
(S) Systems	DFS		DMS	
(T) Transformation	DFT			
(I) Implications	DFI		DMI	

His tests of creativity for children are made up of 10 tasks each measuring one of 10 of the 24 Divergent Production Abilities. The names of these tasks are "Names for Stories," "What to Do With It?," "Similar Meanings," "Writing Sentences," "Kinds of People," "Making Something Out of It," "Different Groups," "Making Objects," "Hidden Letters," and "Adding Decorations." Tasks 1 through 5 are verbal and tasks 6 through 10 are nonverbal.

Verbal Tasks

Names for Stories (Divergent Semantic Units or DMU) The plot of a story is given with a few sample titles. The child is asked to give as many titles as possible in the few minutes given to him. A score is then given for the total number of acceptable clever and nonclever titles. For example:

> One day three friends found a box of gold coins. As they did not want others to know about it they decided to wait for nightfall before taking it into the nearby village. One of them went for food and drink while the two remained to watch over the gold and each other. Soon after they planned to kill their friend when he returned so that each could have more gold coins. The man who went for food and drink wanted all the money for himself, so he put poison in the wine. On his return his two friends attacked and killed him. They then ate the food and drank the wine and soon died. Whatever became of the box of gold coins no one knows to this day.

Riches make men bad.
The lost treasure.
Gold is poison.
False friends.
Death wins after all.

What To Do with It? (Divergent Semantic Classes or DMC) This task is very similar to the Unusual or Alternate Uses task used earlier to illustrate the meaning of flexibility. It requires shifts in thinking and has been described by Guilford as "spontaneous flexibility." It is an ability to produce many different ideas and can aid a person in finding fresh ways of looking at a problem in order to solve it. Ideas produced are given credit if they are unusual (that is, if they do not fall in the class of common use). For example,

A pencil is used for writing, but it could also be used as:
| an arrow |
| firewood |
| pillar for a doll's house |
| toothpick |

Similar Meanings (Divergent Semantic Relations or DMR) The child is required to produce similar meanings for a given word like "fun" or "bad." It calls for the ability to produce alternative relations, and in the adult form it is called Associational Fluency. Guilford observes this kind of ability to be useful in identifying relations in science and in detective work where seeing relations among alternative solutions for a suitable decision to be made is needed. Acceptable meanings are given credit.

Writing Sentences (Divergent Semantic System or DMS) This task deals with the ability to think of alternate ways of organizing some basic information. Several words are given and the child is encouraged to write sentences. Each sentence receives credit if it contains a subject and predicate, uses two of the given words, makes sense, and does not repeat the same organized idea given in the sentence before. For example,

KNIFE   DOG   STICK   BONE   DAVE

| Dave tied his knife to a pole to make a spear. |
| The dog crunched the bone. |
| The lost knife was found by the dog. |
| Dave flung the bone into the pool. |

Kinds of People (Divergent Semantic Implication or DMI) A picture of a commonly known object is given to the child who is told to write down the kinds of jobs people do as suggested by the picture. For instance,

TREE

| **lumberjack** |
| **forester** |
| **botanist** |
| **gardner** |

Nonverbal Tasks

Make Something Out of It (Divergent Figural Units or DFU) This task is similar to the first verbal task, Names for Stories, except that figures or shapes are given to the child who is asked to list the different things that can be made by adding something to each of them. The ability involves the ease with which ideas are produced. The ideas given must relate to the given shape with no credit given for repetitions. For example,

| **leaf** |
| **buttonhole** |
| **spear head** |
| **mouth of a jar** |

Different Letter Groups (Divergent Figural Classes or DFC) The child is given the task of grouping and regrouping three capital letters that are alike in some way taken from six letters given. For example,

C   I   F   L   G   Z

| ILZ (have a base line) |
| IFL (have up-and-down lines) |
| FLZ (a line going across) |
| CIZ (not alike) |

The child is required to use his ability to make classes when given certain units of information, an ability that is very useful when it comes to recalling information from memory storage, where the search involves screening classes rather than units of information. One point is given for every new class of three letters made.

Making Objects (Divergent Figural Systems or DFS) A child is given the task of putting together simple figures or lines to make different things or objects. It is an ability often used by artists, designers, architects, and engineers when they create their products. Credit is given for combining more than one figure to make different objects with changes in size and position and minor changes in the given shapes allowed. For example,

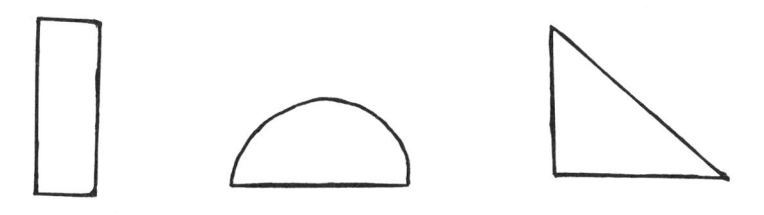

Man	Car	Face in Window

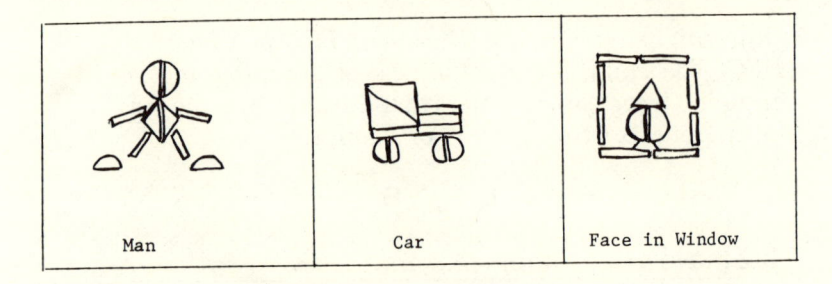

Hidden Letters (Divergent Figural Transformation or DFI) A page of repeated and somewhat complex figures is given to the child. He is to find letters of the alphabet hidden in each of them. This ability requires the child to tear down the lines that make the figure and recombine a few of them into a letter of the alphabet, an ability to transform information that is commonly known into something original. Many inventions have resulted from the use of this kind of ability. Each nonrepeated capital letter so obtained receives credit. For example,

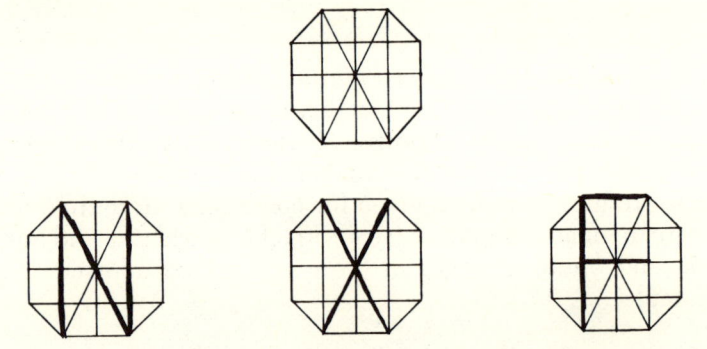

Adding Decorations (Divergent Figural Implication or DFI) This task consists of giving the child drawings of familiar objects like clothing or furniture to which the child is told to add details or to decorate, an ability related to seeing the implications involved, the kind of work an artist or inventor does in adding refinements to a product made. A score is obtained by awarding credit to decorative ideas that are not repeated. For example,

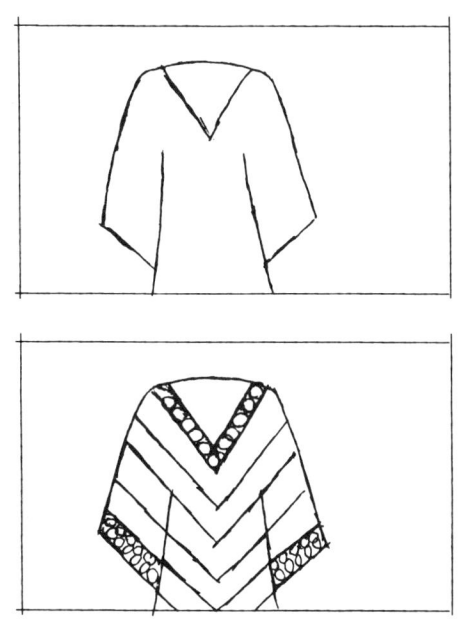

Test Climate

Guilford says that the child needs to feel he is among friends when he is doing the tasks, that the child should be told that doing the tasks is like playing familiar games, that what he is doing has nothing to do with school grades, and that just as in a game, no one will fail. So he should prepare to enjoy himself.

TORRANCE TESTS OF CREATIVE THINKING

Torrance Tests of Creative Thinking relate to the measurement of the four creative thinking abilities described before, namely fluency, flexibility, originality, and elaboration.

The tests are made up of alternate forms of two tests that he has called *Thinking Creatively with Words* and *Thinking Creatively with Pictures*. The tasks in them were made to be interesting and challenging for children and adults from preschool age up. The tests can be given individually or in groups. For the verbal tasks young children dictate their responses to adults and older children write their responses down (Torrance, 1968, 1974).

Verbal Tasks

Ask-and-Guess tasks are the first three of seven tasks that make up the verbal test. They are included to allow for the expression of curiosity and to assess the ability to make hypotheses and think of many possibilities. A picture is given to a person who is encoureaged to ask questions about what is happening in the picture, to guess causes or give reasons for what is taking place, and to guess consequences or the results of the action, all of which could not be answered by merely looking at the picture.

Product Improvement is a complex task that allows a person to play with ideas that he would not dare to express in a more serious situation. The task encourages the participant to think of the most interesting unusual and imaginative ideas to improve a stuffed toy animal to make it more fun to play with. For example:

If you would like to find out what kind of thinking is involved in this test write down as many ways as you can to improve the stuffed toy dog. Give yourself 2½ minutes though in the actual test 10 minutes is allowed. Then take a look at the list of commonplace or zero originality responses listed at the end of this section.

Unusual Uses task is very much like Guilford's Brick Uses Test. It consists of asking the person taking the test to think of unusual, interesting, and seldom thought of uses of a common object such as junk autos. The task requires a person to break away from the set of common uses of the object.

To find out how well you can do on this task, list as many interesting and unusual uses of junk autos as you can in two and one-half minutes. Then look at the list of common or unoriginal responses that are scored zero, given at the end of this section to check your responses.

Unusual Questions task is based on a method used to measure "divergent power," which is considered essential for creative achievement and critical for creativity in the classroom. The task encourages a person to ask questions that are novel and unusual.

Just Suppose task is like Guilford's consequences type test and is a variation of the second task of this test, namely, Guess Consequences. The task is designed to elicit a higher degree of fantasy and is expected to work very well with children. A person is asked to think of all the possible things that could take place if something not likely to happen did happen. For instance, "Just suppose it was raining and all the drops stood still in the air and wouldn't move—and they were solid." Each *Just Suppose* task is accompanied by an interesting drawing depicting the improbable situation.

You might like to try this task too, giving yourself two and one-half minutes, and then check to see if you have uncommon responses by looking at the list of common or unoriginal responses at the end of this section.

Nonverbal or Figural Tasks

Picture Construction Activity. A shape such as a tear drop or jelly bean made of colored paper with a sticky back is given to a person. He is told to use it as an important part of a picture he is about to make, and to which he is encouraged to add details to give it more meaning. This task is expected to set in motion the tendency toward finding a purpose for something that has no definite purpose and to elaborate on it in such a way that the purpose is achieved.

Incomplete Figures. This task is based on the theory that the incompleteness of a figure arouses in a person tensions to complete it in the simplest and easiest way possible. Thus if an original picture is to be produced, a person usually has to control his tensions and delay the joy of completing the picture. The task consists of 10 incomplete figures accompanied by the following instructions:

> By adding lines to figures on this and the next page, you can sketch some interesting objects or pictures. Again, try to think of some picture or object that no one else will think of. Try to make it tell as complete and as interesting a story as you can by adding to and building up your first idea. Make up a title for each of your drawings and write it at the bottom of each block next to the number of the figure.

You might like to test yourself with these two figures and compare your responses with the list given at the end of the section to see if you were able to get away from common or unoriginal responses.

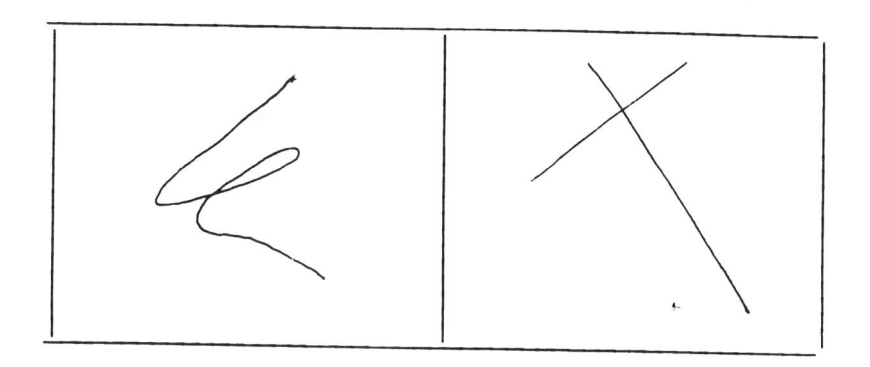

Repeated Figures. Just like the Incomplete Figures task, the Repeated Figures task gives a person two or three pages of closed figures, such as triangles and lines, with the encouragement to use his imagination to create pictures using the triangles or lines as important parts of them. In theory, the lines are supposed to arouse the creative tendency to bring structure and completeness to what is incomplete, while the triangles require the ability to disrupt or destroy an already complete form.

If you wish to try this task, draw on a sheet of paper six rows of four triangles each, and follow the instructions giving yourself 2½ minutes although 10 minutes is allowed for the actual task. Uncommon or unoriginal responses are listed at the end of this section as well for your information.

In two and one-half minutes see how many objects or pictures you can make from the triangles . . . . The triangles should be the main part of whatever you make. With pencil or crayon add lines to the triangles to complete your picture. You can place marks inside them, on them, and outside them—whatever you want to do in order to make your picture. Try to think of things that no one else will think of. Make as many different pictures or objects as you can and put as many ideas as you can in each one. Make them tell as complete and as interesting a story as you can.

Test Climate

Torrance recommends that a game-like, thinking, or problem-solving atmosphere be created; that the person taking the test does not feel threatened, but rather encouraged to enjoy the activities; and that the psychological climate both before and during the tests should be as comfortable and stimulating as possible. As the "warm-up" process is necessary for creative behavior, the cover of the test booklet with its apparently unrelated combinations of elements that usually evokes curiosity, imaginative activity, and interest is designed to facilitate this. This feature the author considers an essential part of the testing procedure.

THINKING CREATIVELY WITH SOUNDS AND WORDS

Two tests of verbal originality, *Sounds and Images* (Cunnington and Torrance, 1965a) and *Onomatopoeia and Images* (Khatena, 1971a) make up the measure *Thinking Creatively with Sounds and Words* (Torrance, Khatena, and Cunnington, 1973). While *Sounds and Images* provides sounds, *Onomatopoeia and Images* provides onomatopoeic words as stimuli to the person taking the test. Both measures call for free association to produce original verbal images that are scored for originality in the way described earlier in the chapter. The measures invite the use of the creative imagination to make a break away from the set of the obvious and commonplace created by the sounds or onomatopoeic words so as to produce original verbal images.

Sounds and Images

In *Sounds and Images*, three repetitions of a group of four recorded audio effects are presented, interspersed with narrated instructions that in effect force the listener to reject commonplace associations for free-wheeling, imaginative ideas. The test relies upon the simple to the complex and from the common to the unusual to evoke original verbal images. Each form of the test presents both single and multiple sound sets. Forms 1A and 1B are the Children's Version of the measure. The first reaction to the presentation of the sounds often results in the production of stereotyped or common responses. Considerable creative power is needed by the participant to break away from the usual sequence of thought into an altogether different pattern of thought often requiring the power of synthesis (where several sounds must be combined into a thought as a whole) to produce the original. Here is an excerpt of the recorded narrative (Demonstration Record):

Have you ever given much thought to the world of sound, that mysterious region just beyond your eardrums? It's as close as the ring of your telephone, the rustle of wind through the trees in your backyard, or the rumble of thunder on a warm summer afternoon.

In just a moment you're going to take a journey into the most fantastic corners of that world . . . and there hear things you've never heard before. Although the first sound you'll meet along the way should be familiar enough the others are going to seem somewhat strange to your ears, and you'll most likely scratch your head a bit as you wonder what on earth they might be.

On this journey you're going to listen to four separate sounds. As you listen to each sound, attempt to picture it in your mind's eye, and then try to write a short description of it on the page before you . . . .

As you listen to the sounds, be sure to use every last bit of imagination you possess while you write down the word pictures they call to your mind. Chances are the sounds will also call up a host of different feelings within you. Try to capture these feelings as they come to you, and hold onto them until you've written them down. Remember, write down your impression of each sound as it occurs in the recording . . . All set? Here we go, then, into the mysterious world of sound . . . .

Onomatopoeia and Images

Onomatopoeia and Images presents auditory-visual stimuli in the form of onomatopoeic words like "crunch" or "tingle." These words have meaning and sound elements that have many layers of meaning both relating to the fact itself and to other facts with feeling content established through usage. The onomatopoeic words, when presented to the listener, act as sets (that is, cause the listener to think of common or usual meanings of the word) from which he must break away by using what Coleridge refers to as the more conscious and less elemental secondary imagination to produce new or unusual combinations of meaning. The sound component of these words subtly strikes the listener unaware, stirring his emotions so that he will tend to think of unusual imaginative meanings in response to what he hears. The creative process works best to produce original thoughts when both the intellect and emotions are involved.

Just as in *Sounds and Images*, the test is administered in standard conditions by presenting all instructions on long-playing records. A narrator prepares the subject by explaining the nature and purpose of the test and calling him to use his creative imagination to produce original verbal images. Five onomatopoeic words for the Children's Version or Forms 1A and 1B are read four times. After the first, second, and third readings of the onomatopoeic words, the narrator encourages the listener to use his imagination to produce more original verbal images than before. Here is an excerpt of the recorded narrative (Demonstration Record):

Do you know that some words are quite musical? You can tell their meanings by their sounds. They can stir your feelings to make you happy or sad, kind, or cruel. They can make you behave in a certain way even when you do not know their meanings.

Musical words seem to have a certain magic, and together with your imagination they can make you think in the way a poet does when he writes a poem or an inventor when he makes something entirely new.

So that you too can show how well you can set your imagination to work, a list of musical words has been given to you. All you have to do is to listen carefully to the words as they are spoken, and by using your imagination try to picture in your mind what you think no one else would have thought of. For example, listen to this word . . . "blast." The picture you get at first may be of some kind of explosion, like a bomb explosion, setting off a charge of dynamite, a jet plane taking off or a volcanic eruption. But anyone could have thought of those. How about you? Listen to the words as they are spoken and each time try to think of a new picture to write about . . .

. . . Remember to use your imagination to help you think of interesting and unusual pictures to write about. Are you ready?

Some Helping Conditions

While *Sounds and Images* presents stimuli in the form of sound sets and *Onomatopoeia and Images* presents stimuli in the form of onomatopoeic word sets, both have certain built-in conditions that assist the listener in allowing the freedom of imagination to create original images. Both tests use progressive warm-up, make divergent thinking legitimate, provide freedom from the threat of evaluation, invite regression, and aid the breaking of inhibiting sound and word sets.

Test Climate

The authors of the test consider it essential that good rapport be established before the administration of the test. The examiner should attempt to create a nontest atmosphere where a person can feel that he is about to have some fun using his imagination.

OTHER INFORMATION ABOUT THE GUILFORD AND TORRANCE MEASURES

These tests have been successfully used to measure the divergent or creative thinking abilities of children and adults. Guilford's tests of creativity for children have been normed for children between grades 4 and 6, although they may also be used with children in the other grades. Torrance's figural measures have been used with children of all groups from preschool to grade 12, as well as with adults. His verbal measures come in two forms. There is a kit for individual administration to children from preschool to grade 2 when the examiner has to write the responses children give, although the test kit may also be used with children in other grades if required. The test kit is made up of the first four activities of the booklet form of the measure described previously. namely, the three Ask and Guess activities, and the Product Improvement activity. The booklet form of the verbal test generally used for group administration contains all the verbal activities described previously, and has been used with children from grades 3 and up as well as with adults. The responses are written by the children themselves. *Thinking Creatively With Sounds and Words* has been used with children between grades 3 and 12 and adults.

If you need to know your child's divergent or creative thinking abilities, you should go to a psychologist and ask him to use one of these measures. You will not be able to obtain these measures for your personal use unless you have had some training in psychological testing. Even if you were able to get them it would be better to get the services of someone who has had the training to administer the test to your child, score it and explain the results to you, and probably even advise what you can do with the information given to you.

LIST OF COMMON, UNORIGINAL RESPONSES TO DEMONSTRATOR FORM

(ZERO CREDIT FOR ORIGINALITY)

1. *Ask Questions*
   How can it run connected only to wooden drawers?
   Why is it plugged into chest/table?
   Why is the fan blowing?
   Why is it on the chest of drawers?
   Who is he (man)?
   Is he a teacher?
   Whom is he speaking/talking to?
   What is he pointing at?
   What is he talking about?
   Why is he pointing to the fan?
   What/what kind of machine is it?
   What are the levers/buttons, etc.?
   What do the lines represent?
   What is in the drawers?
2. *Product Improvement* (Toy Dog)
   Bark, make it

Bell, add on neck, feet, etc.
Bow, add
Color, add or change
Cuddly, make it
Ears, bigger, longer
Eyes, bigger, move, wink, sparkle, glow, etc.
Face, give expression personality
Fluffy, more like real fur
Fuzzy, make
Larger, longer, taller, etc.; legs longer
Mouth, bigger
Movable parts at joints
Music box inside
Noise, have him make
Nose, bigger
Paws, add, make bigger, etc.
Realistic, make
Ribbon, add brighter color, bigger bow, etc.
Smile, make
Softer
Tail, curl up, make longer
Tongue, longer

3. *Unusual Uses* (Junk Autos)
Art, abstract, modern sculpture, pop art
Autos, make one from several
Autos, play on playground
Chairs
Demolition derby
Demonstration, warning for drivers
Educational uses, rebuild to learn, give to teenagers to learn about cars
Flower planter
Playground, pretend cars
Racing
Repair to sell
Scrap iron, metal, etc.
Spare parts, see for use on other cars
Swing, tires used for

    Tension reducer, smash with hammer
    Tires, recap and sell
    Toy on playground
4. *Just Suppose* (Rain Still and Solid)
    No water
    No grass, no leaves on trees, no flowers, no plant life
    People would be bumping into them
    Earth would be parched
    No fish to catch
    Sunshiny, no clouds in sky
    No travelling
    Airplanes could not fly
    Couldn't take a bath
    No boating, swimming, etc.
    No floods
    No need for raincoats
    Animals would die
    No rivers, creeks, etc.
5. *Incomplete Figures* (Figures in Two Squares)
    Figure, left:
    Abstract figure
    Bird(s)
    Human (man, woman, child)
    Figure, right:
    Abstract figure
    Horse head or horse body
    House
    Kite
6. *Repeated Triangles*
    Amorphous, indistinct figure
    Cottage, house, etc.
    Design
    Human face
    Human figure (man, woman, child)
    Star (six-point)
    Tent, tepee
    Tree
    Triangle

4: An Instrument For Parents and Teachers

When I began developing *Something About Myself* (1971b) on the basis of some earlier research with creativity checklists, I conceived the need for a measure to identify creative talent that would not be too long, could be easily and rapidly administered and scored by people with very little or no training in measurement, and could be interpreted by people who were able to understand what was being measured and for what purpose.

I recognized that few parents and teachers have direct access to instruments that would help them appropriately identify the creative talent of their children for purposes of help at home, special grouping and educational experiences in the classroom or school, like the instruments described in the chapter before. That you have had to rely solely on psychologists for information about your children's abilities seemed to me to place you in a position of definite disadvantage. An instrument that was designed for your use, I felt, would allow you not only to derive the information you needed almost at once, but also to understand what the instrument was doing and so put you in a better position to use the information you derived.

A few years ago I had talked to a parent group at the

Community Health Center in Huntington, West Virginia, about the creatively gifted child and the role parents could play to facilitate the child's educational development. It was at this time that I clearly saw a way to help them to get over some of the helplessness they feel in trying to figure out if their children are creatively gifted.

This reminds me of a letter a distressed parent wrote some years ago to the Editor of the *Gifted Child Quarterly* seeking advice about her twenty-two-month-old daughter whom she suspected to be gifted:

> My daughter, who is now twenty-two months old, had a vocabulary of four hundred words at eighteen months. She now speaks in sentences. She has a remarkable memory, long span of attention, and an eagerness to learn. She has great physical coordination, is creative, and very independent.
>
> Are there any guidelines by which I can determine if she is gifted? Is she too young to be tested? If she is old enough, where would it be done, by whom, and how much would it cost? If she is not gifted, how can I help her develop her quick learning abilities? If she is gifted, at what age could formal training begin and what can I do to help until then? (Pippin, 1967.)

This kind of anxiety is not uncommon to sensitive parents who want the best for their children, and some of the evidence in the first chapter of this book supports this still further.

To continue with what I was saying about the parent group at the Mental Health Center, I then suggested that using an instrument like *Something About Myself* would give them the right kind of clues about creatively gifted children.

SOMETHING ABOUT MYSELF

Something About Myself is one of two tests named the *Khatena-Torrance Creative Perception Inventory* (Khatena and Torrance, 1976), and the other is *What Kind of Person are You?* Both measures have been designed for adolescents and adults although they may be administered to younger people with the help of an adult.

Something About Myself is based upon the rationale that creativity can show itself in personality traits, in the way a person thinks, and in the products that a person makes. It is made up of 50 items which can be easily given and interpreted by a parent or teacher. Scoring the test is done just by counting the number of "Yes" answers given with the total number of "Yes" answers providing a creative perception index of the person.

To give you an idea of what you will find in *Something About Myself*, here are a few sample items of the measure:

——I am an imaginative person, a dreamer or visionary.
——When I think of an idea I like adding to it to make it more interesting.
——I have improvised in dance, song or instrumental music.
——I am not afraid to take risks should a need arise.
——I have invented a new product.

In addition to the creative perception index, the measure gives six creative orientations, namely: Environmental Sensitivity, Initiative, Self Strength, Intellectuality, Individuality, and Artistry.

Environmental Sensitivity

A person who is Environmentally Sensitive considers the ideas of others as well as his own; relates ideas to what can be seen, touched or heard; is interested in the beautiful and humorous aspects of experiences; and likes to know others in a meaningful way.

Initiative

A person who is high on Initiative directs, produces, and/or plays lead roles in dramatic and musical productions; produces new formulas or products, and brings about changes in procedures or organization.

Self-Strength

A person who has Self-Strength possesses self-confidence in matching talents against others; is resourceful, versatile and willing to take risks; has the desire to excel; and has organization ability.

Intellectuality

A person who shows high on Intellectuality has intellectual curiosity; who enjoys challenging tasks; who has imagination and preference for adventure over routine; who likes reconstructing things and ideas to form something different; and who dislikes doing things in a prescribed and routine way.

Individuality

A person who has Individuality prefers to work alone rather than in a group; who sees himself as a self-starter; who is eccentric; who is critical of others; who thinks for himself; and who works for long periods without getting tired.

Artistry

A person who has Artistry produces objects, models, paintings and carvings; who composes music; who has been awarded prizes or has had his works exhibited; and who has produced stories, plays, poems and other literary pieces.

CRITERIA FOR IDENTIFICATION, DIAGNOSIS, AND FACILITATION

From an experiment I had done a few years ago on effects of training children between the ages of 5 and 11 years to think creatively with pictures, I found that not all children at every stage of their lives need to be taught with the same intensity how to think productively, and that it would be of value to provide training where and when it is needed or to nurture specific talents: in this way children who need help can be given it at once.

This leads me to suggest a plan that will help you deal with both the identification and nurture issues together, with the emphasis not on identification but on diagnosis directed towards facilitation of the creative potential of children. That is to say, we need to set up some criteria to determine strengths and weaknesses in creative functioning and then go on to arrange for experiences that will increase the chances of children to act in creative ways according to the criteria set.

A FOUR-STEP PLAN OF ACTION

One set of criteria may be found ready-made in *Something About Myself* that may be used for identification, diagnosis and facilitation. I am suggesting a four-step plan as follows: (Khatena, 1977a, 220-221)

1. Administer the measure to your child or student: if he needs your help to respond to statements relative to the measure, give the help needed.
2. Score the measure to determine the child or student's creative perception index and scores on the six creative orientations. To do this you will have to refer to the scoring manual of the measure.
3. Identify the child or student's strengths and weaknesses by observing the direction of items checked individually, and within each of the six creative orientations.
4. With this information you are now in a position to decide what to do for each child according to his special needs. As back-up to this you should have prepared creative activities and situations either of your own composition or the composition of others like those proposed by Renzulli (1973) or Williams (1971).

SOME CLUES ABOUT CREATIVE PERCEPTIONS

A recent study explored the developmental patterns and creative orientations of a large group of adolescent and adult West Virginians (Khatena, 1975) and found (1) that in general the creative perceptions of adolescent boys and girls as measured by the total scale were lower than those of college men and women; (2) that boys and men showed somewhat better on the scale than girls and women; (3) that relative to the six creative orientations, generally, both adolescents and adults were found to be very high on Environmental Sensitivity but very low on Initiative, and (4) that the remaining four orientations appear in the following order of importance, namely, Intellectuality, Individuality, Self-Strength, and Artistry.

These findings tell us that as adolescents grow older and become adults their creative activities in the world are likely to increase both in number and complexity. So if their creative activities and personality dimensions can be identified early enough, then those creative activities and personality dimensions which they do not show initially can be encouraged through experiences we plan for them.

If a person were to be screened by *Something About Myself*, an analysis of his responses on each of the items relative to creative personality characteristics, thinking operations, and productions will provide information for arrangements of experiences that will facilitate his creative development. In addition, his responses to the whole scale can be regrouped to show how he fares on the six creative orientations. The study just described suggests that some educational experiences may have to be provided for the development of Initiative since this is the orientation in which a person seems to be most deficient.

Another study (Khatena, 1974) reported the use of *Something About Myself* as a diagnostic tool for program development for talented and gifted children, and as a screening device to determine how parents perceived their children's creative development. What emerged from the analyses of the data were helpful clues about the relative strengths and weaknesses of these gifted students' creative perceptions. In particular the creative orientations of Environmental Sensitivity and Intellectuality tend to be their greatest strengths, while Initiative tends to be their greatest weakness with Self-Strength, Individuality, and Artistry spread in the middle. These findings are supported by evidence of the earlier study on development.

The findings of this study with talented and gifted students, led to recommendations for the next phase of program development for them. Provision was to be made for the inclusion of planned experiences that would strengthen in particular the lacks relative to Initiative in terms of opportunity for students to direct or produce plays or skits, to take part in lead roles in dramatic or musical productions, to produce formulas, to make things, and even to practice the sensing of deficiencies in procedural patterns and organizations for the purpose of suggesting improvements, and other leadership roles that go beyond the screening instrument.

Another creative orientation that was to be strengthened was Artistry since this was the next lowest in the scale of creative perceptions. This would involve gifted students in the production of objects, models, paintings, and carvings; creative writing of stories, plays, poems, and other literary pieces; and arranging for recognition of these efforts by way of exhibition and prizes (Khatena, 1977a, 222).

Both studies tell us that although our children may see themselves as creative in many ways, they tend not to see themselves as having leadership roles or as engaging in artistic pursuits. We have great need for creative leaders, and it may be that if we provide our children with appropriate leadership experiences early, some fine creative leaders will emerge in the future to the benefit of all. Further, the continued emphasis on science over the past few decades has allowed the arts to recede in importance. Achievements in science complemented by accomplishments in the arts will allow humankind to transcend itself. That is why it is important for us to provide early experiences of creative composition and performances in art, music, drama, poetry, and other forms of creative expression. As parents and teachers you can do much to arrange for relevant experiences at home and in the classroom that will encourage the development of leadership qualities and artistic talent.

AN INSTANCE OF THE MODEL AT WORK

Let me focus your attention as well on some of the items of the checklist that refer to the creative process—ones with which I have successfully worked in experiments and which you can use with children specific to their needs as explained in the next few paragraphs (Khatena, 1977a, 223-224).

Take for example item 9 of the checklist: "I like breaking

down something organized in a certain way into its components parts and reorganize it in a different way to make it into something no one else would have thought of." Briefly, this operation can be described as *restructuring*, and some information about it and how you can make it work for your child is given as follows:

We are often faced with something whose parts are put together or structured in a certain way to give it an identity. If we are able to pull apart these elements and recombine them or restructure them in a different way we are very likely to come up with something having a new or original identity. It really needs creative energy to free oneself from the bonds of the old order for the purpose of bringing about a new order.

1. *Restructuring Using Nonverbal or Figural Materials*

To teach your child to use this strategy with figural materials you may start with constructing an 8 x 12 inch flannel-board, and make cutouts of say 3 geometrical shapes such that you have 10 of each kind. I have preferred to use black flannel to cover the board, and some brightly colored, lightweight paper-board for the geometrical shapes like the semicircle, triangle, and rectangle. If you like to use these shapes, make circles one inch in diameter and squares that have sides one inch long. By cutting the circles in two you will get semicircles, and by cutting the square into four parts you will have rectangles; in addition you can make two right-angled triangles by cutting across the diagonal of a square. These shapes are relatively versatile and allow for all kinds of manipulations and combinations. When you have all these pieces cut, put them in a little plastic bag or envelope ready for use. You should make two sets so that you can freely work with your child on the materials.

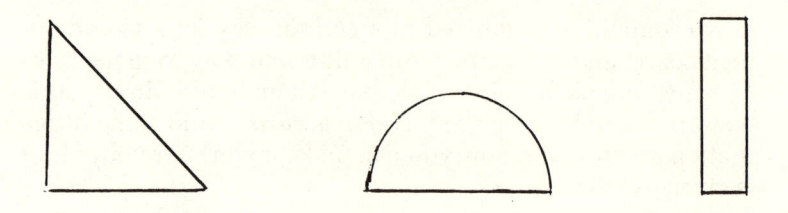

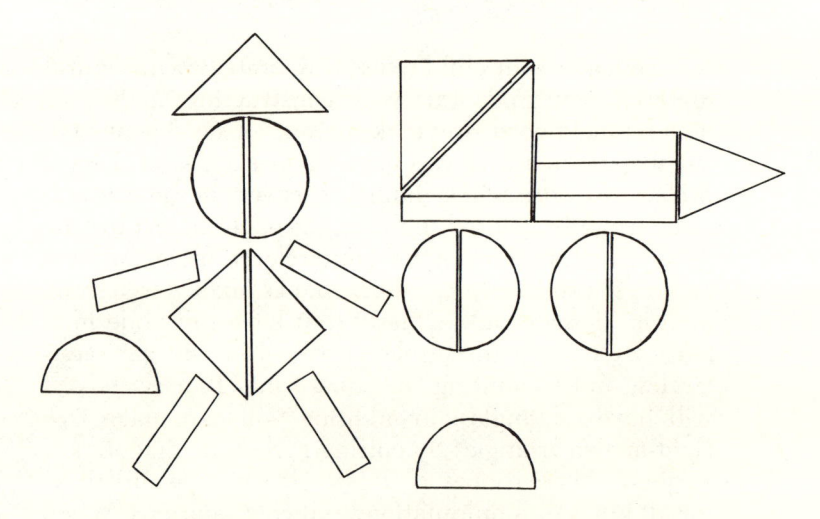

Now that these pieces are ready and the flannel-board prepared, give them to your child. Tell him that you are going to construct a figure on the flannel-board and get him to watch what you do. You may begin by constructing a *human figure*: a triangle for a hat, two semicircles for the face, two triangles for the body, two rectangles for the arms and two more for the legs, and two semicircles for the feet. All this requires the use of 3 triangles, 4 semicircles and 4 rectangles, making a total of 11 pieces. Encourage your child to do the same giving him whatever help he may need at the time. Then pull apart the pieces you used to make the human figure and reconstruct them into an *automobile* making sure that only the same 11 pieces are used. The four semicircles can now serve as the two wheels. Place one rectangle on one wheel and a second rectangle on the other so that the long sides of the two rectangles are on the wheels and the short sides are side by side. Then place two triangles in the shape of a square upon the rectangles on the rear wheel, and the remaining two rectangles upon the one that was first placed on the front wheel. Finally put the remaining triangle against the short sides of the three rectangles above the front wheel so that its base is against them and the apex of the triangle is pointing forward. The car is now ready. Let your child do the same and once again help him to build the car. When he has done this tell him to pull apart the same 11 parts of the automobile and rearrange or restructure them into another object. Of course with a little practice you will see him producing scenes as well. Your child may try to persuade you to allow him to use some of the pieces in the bag but do not let him. Encourage him to use his imagination and work within the restrictions of the strategy.

2. *Restructuring Using Verbal-Figural Materials*

Restructuring can also be used to encourage your child to be more creative with words. For instance, you can show him a picture of the Three Wise Men of Gotham and encourage him to ask questions about it which cannot be answered by merely looking at the picture, guess why events in the scene are taking place, and the consequences of these events, as warm-up activities. This may then be followed by getting him to restructure three elements of the picture, namely, the three wise men, the bowl, and the sea, into an unusual and interesting story.

What I have proposed in this chapter is an Identification Diagnostic Facilitation Model that will lend itself to determine the specific needs of children for nurture, so that some kind of precision can enter into the formulation of strategies aimed at facilitating the education of the gifted. It is a model (1) whose identification component can be used in its own right if needed by both parent and teacher who hitherto have had to depend upon psychological services for measurement and interpretation, and (2) whose nurture component immediately keeps open-ended the selection of activities by parent or teacher relative to the specific needs of the child, thus getting around the problem of a broadside program attack leveled at all children irrespective of their needs.

Some of the things you can do to stimulate your children's creative thinking are also described in the next chapter. In addition I have suggested other useful materials at the end of the book that you can obtain to help you do this.

5: Some Activities to Stimulate Creative Thinking

From a recent Federal Government Report (Marland, 1972) and several other sources, we learn about some of the better learning opportunities that have been provided for gifted and talented children. Generally these have taken the form of the following:

enrichment of the curriculum materials and physical surroundings;
more effective ways of teaching and learning;
psychological climates that are conducive to learning;
providing correspondence courses and tutoring;
placing high school students in advanced grades or classes;
arranging for gifted high school students to attend college classes;
giving special counsel or instruction outside classrooms;
providing sensitivity training;
individualizing instruction by way of team teaching, nongraded plans, independent study and the like;
arranging for highly gifted students to attend special classes and work with specially trained teachers, supervisors and consultants;

arranging for them to work in special groups, improving the curriculum through programs that emphasize higher level thought processes, creativity and divergent thinking; and

giving special attention to the emotional and social adjustment of gifted pupils.

About 20 years of study has given us considerable evidence that we can do much to assist people generally and gifted children in particular, to use their creative abilities more often and in better ways. Torrance (1972) has recently summarized about 142 of these studies that attempt to teach children to be more creative by using several different approaches such as:

programs emphasizing the Osborn-Parnes Creative Problem-Solving procedures;
programs involving packages of materials such as the Purdue Creativity Program;
the creative arts as vehicles for teaching and practicing creative thinking;
media and reading programs designed to teach and give practice in creative thinking;
curricular and administrative arrangements designed to create favorable conditions for learning and practicing creative thinking;
teacher-classroom variables, indirect and direct control, classroom climate, and the like;
motivation, reward, competition, and the like; and
testing conditions designed to facilitate a higher level of creative functioning or more valid and reliable test performance.

To these must be added some recent applications of creative thinking operations and creative problem-solving techniques that can be used to train people to think ahead and anticipate problems that they will need to solve in the future in creative ways.

STIMULATING THE CREATIVE IMAGINATION

My work has focused on several dimensions of the creative imagination and its stimulation by the creative thinking strategies of Breaking Away from the Usual and Commonplace, Restructuring, and Synthesis of children to express themselves more creatively. I have looked upon these strategies as ways to encourage the use of figural or nonverbal imagery and verbal imagery to which may be added the several forms of analogy (Khatena, 1977b, 86-93).

Breaking Away From the Usual and Commonplace and Analogy

The thinking strategy breaking away from the usual and commonplace or what is sometimes known as breaking away from perceptual set can be illustrated by presenting the child with the figural stimulus "square" followed by two drawings or figural analogies, namely a window and a clock, and he can be told that if he used the square to make these drawings, then he would be doing things the way he always did them. Other common drawings may be barn, blackboard, book, door, and flag. However, if he drew a large enough circle around the square to make, say a bubble with the square as highlight, he would be using his imagination to get away from older habits of thought.

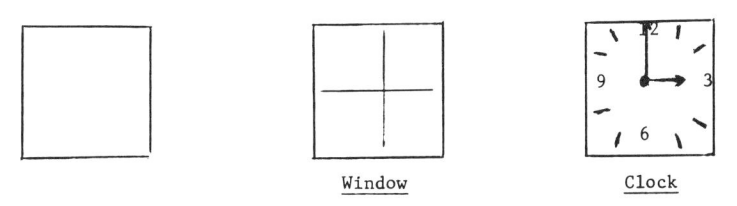

Window   Clock

Exercise 1 You can then give him a worksheet containing four rows of three squares each and encourage him to draw interesting and unusual pictures using the square. You will be amazed to see him producing all kinds of interesting figural analogies from, say earphones to Martians in Mexico. All along, show you appreciate his attempts, and if he really moves away from drawing objects like window or door which are dependent on angular constructions do not forget to praise him.

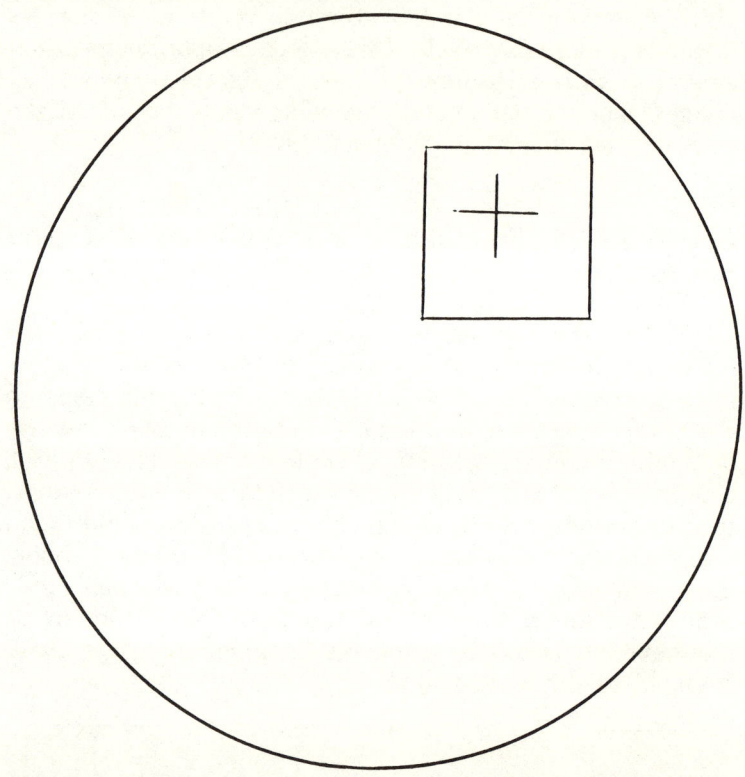

Exercise 2 A second exercise could involve circles as the figural stimulus for the production of creative analogies and images. You can give the child a worksheet containing three rows of five circles each. Tell him to look at each circle in turn, close his eyes and think of an object it suggests (that is, an image), draw the picture or image that takes its life from the circle, add details to give it more meaning (that is, make

simple—complex figural images), and have him create pictures or figural images that are not entirely circular (for example, port hole of a ship, or round mirror). If he does this he has been able to break away from the obvious and commonplace. Do encourage him to use his imagination and do appreciate his attempts.

Other shapes like the triangle and ellipse may be used in the same way as well.

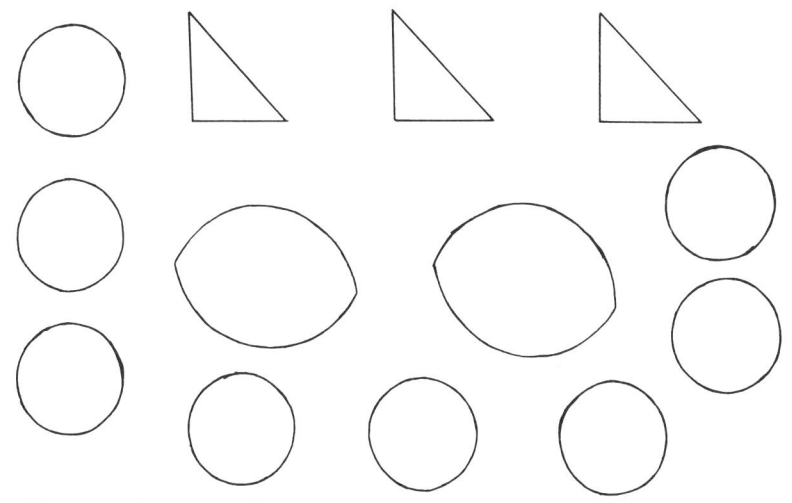

Exercise 3 As another example, you may give the child the onomatopoeic stimulus word "roar" with instructions to be imaginative in responding to it. If the child produces verbal analogies like "to talk noisily" or "the sound a lion makes" you may regard these as commonplace, whereas an analogy like "blood gushing out of a wound" is imaginative and shows creative strength and may be regarded as such. Illustrate what you want done and follow it with practice exercises that show the imagination at work. Do not forget to give the child appropriate praise relative to imaginative responses he makes. You may use other onomatopoeic words like "squelch" and "drone" or sounds of one kind or another that you have recorded for the purpose.

Restructuring Images

The second thinking strategy, restructuring, is another method to encourage creative thinking. We are often faced with something whose parts are put together or structured in a certain way to give it an identity. If we are able to pull apart these elements and recombine them or restructure them in a different way we are very likely to come up with some image having new or original identity. It really needs creative energy to free oneself from the bonds of the old order for the purpose of bringing about a new order. In Chapter Four I have also discussed this thinking strategy and suggested how we might teach a child to use this strategy by working with semicircles, triangles, and rectangles on flannel board (pp. in pages). To this exercise may be added the following:

Exercise 1 Another very useful exercise in restructuring figural imagery is to give the student the picture of an airplane constructed of four rectangles, two triangles, and one oval cutout shapes for restructuring as per picture with the following instructions:

> Here is a picture of an airplane which you can pull to pieces and put together again to make the same airplane if you wish. You can also put the pieces together to make something no one else would have thought of. When you have made up your mind as to what you want to do, pull out the pieces and stick them on the next page to make the kind of picture you want. You may also make use of your pencil or crayons to help you. When you have your picture drawn give it a title.

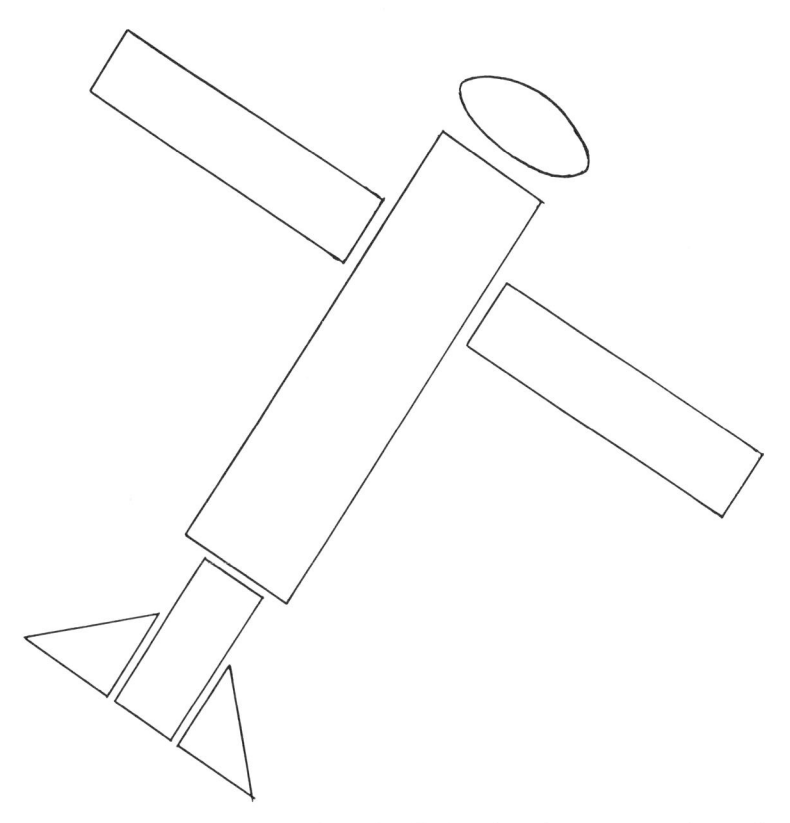

You will see produced all kinds of creative figural images, for instance, a hula dance, house and yard scene, guarding the olympic torch, one-legged ballet dancer, and various abstract ideas illustrating gravity pull, reorientation, balance, and the like. By adding details to the picture or figural image to give it more meaning the child would have transformed the object or scene from the simple to the complex image.

You might also refer to Chapter Four for another exercise that encourages a child to produce verbal images in response to figural image stimuli in terms of a picture of the Three Wise Men of Gotham the elements of which are to be restructured into an unusual and interesting story (p. 59 in text). The story may be enriched by the use of analogies as described in the section on exercises in figures and analogies described later in this chapter.

Synthesizing Images

A third strategy called Synthesis can also be taught to your child. Unlike restructuring, the act of synthesis provides more freedom of manipulation and expression. Your child may be allowed to use as many of the shapes as he likes to produce new and interesting figural images or pictures on the same flannel-board.

Exercise 1 You can begin by demonstrating how the pieces can be combined to make a scene of two boys on a seesaw. Give your child a chance to do the same and encourage him to make as many of his own pictures as he can such that each time he will remember to use his imagination to produce the new and unusual. Encourage and praise him for self-initiated and interesting and unusual combinations.

You may encourage him to use his imagination still further by asking him to talk about the characters and scenes he makes. You may even encourage him to tell a story about them, and if it helps the development of his narrative then suggest or allow him to change details of the scene he has before him.

Exercise 2 Synthesis can also encourage children to be imaginative and produce verbal images to figural image stimuli. For example, you can show your child a picture of Wee Willie Winkie and get him to tell you something about it so that he will ask questions, guess causes and consequences in much the same way that was described for restructuring, all of which require the use of the imagination. A second picture can then be shown of a Schoolmaster and his Student with similar warm-up activities (that is, encourage your child to ask questions about the events which cannot be answered by merely looking at the pictures, guess why events in the scene are taking place, and the consequences of these events). Your child can then be asked to tell a story using a combination of the characters and situations in both pictures with encouragement to use his imagination to make his story unusual and interesting. As in restructuring, the story may be enriched by the use of analogies and figures of speech described later in the chapter.

Exercise 3 In another exercise draw a circle in which you place a number of words, and then ask your child to pick out at least two words from the word pool and combine them together with other words of the child's choosing to make interesting or unusual sentences. You can go on from that to help him use words in the pool to make analogies. He must use at least two of the words from the pool each time, and there is nothing to stop him from using more than two words from the pool if he wishes.

As an illustration, let us take the following word pool from which we will draw words to make analogies as follows:

ruby

pearls eyes teeth

love beauty joy

snow sun moon

lips cheek spring

winter lily

1. The sun turned her lips to ruby red.
2. His smile had the beauty of pearls.
3. The lily under a blanket of snow waited for the sun to stir its roots.

You may follow this up with other word pools similar to these:

waves wind

heart finger head

car spaceship train

dream angel fairy

witch house

empty

angry

fire leaves peanuts

animal ghost superman

rope chains insect

bubble moan

dance

Verbal Analogy, Figures of Speech, and Imagery

We use words with their objective meanings and emotional connotations to convey to others our ideas, feelings, and perceptions about the world. Often we find ourselves trying to communicate thoughts, feelings, or experiences that do not lend themselves to easy expression: we cannot explain or describe what we have in mind; so we search for some familiar situation to which our thought-feeling complex can be related—a process of making the *strange* familiar; sometimes by reversing the process whereby we make the *familiar* strange we allow ourselves insights into relations hitherto concealed to us.

ANALOGY

Both these mechanisms are operations involved in the making of creative analogies and have been presented to us in the Synectics approach to creative problem solving (Gordon, 1961). Synectics distinguishes four kinds of analogies: personal analogy, direct analogy, fantasy analogy, and symbolic analogy.

Personal Analogy

In personal analogy a relationship is found between yourself and some other phenomena with which you and others are familiar. Suppose you want others to know how thin you are without having to give a lengthy description, you may say:

I'm as thin as a stick.

Or suppose you want to tell someone that you are happy, you may say:

I'm as happy as a lark.

Direct Analogy

Just like personal analogy, direct analogy finds a relationship between two unlike phenomena but without self-involvement. To produce a direct analogy, the "I" of the comparison above may become "he" or "John" to read:

John is as thin as a stick.

Another direct analogy relative to being fat could be:

John is as fat as a pig.

And if the activity is focused on his eating habits, the analogy may be:

John eats like a pig.

Symbolic Analogy

This form of analogy uses a symbol where we try to find a "sign" for a phenomenon we wish to describe that has many related characteristics. For instance, if we come across someone who is dependable, strong, stable, consistent, and so on, and we wish to convey this information about him effectively without having to use too many words, we look around for some phenomenon, animate or inanimate which has as nearly as possible these qualities. For example, the "Rock of Gibraltar," has been traditionally known to have such qualities. The "Rock" then can be used as a "sign" or "symbol" of the qualities possessed by the person in mind. We may then refer to him using symbolic analogy as:

He is the Gibraltar of my life.

or

John is as firm as The Rock.

Fantasy Analogy

In fantasy analogy, the comparison object or subject at least must be imaginary. Myths, legends, allegories, fairy tales, and the like are all rich sources of imaginary materials for comparison as for instance, the Devil, Medusa, Pandora's Box, Ariel, the Rainbow, the Dragon, the Garden of Eden, Paradise, Sugar Candy Mountain, Jekyll and Hyde, and so on. Let us say you wish to convey the information that someone we know is very wicked, evil, and murderous. We may compare such a person to Hyde like:

John is Hyde himself.

or

Lenora's whispers stirred the Hyde in John.

IMAGERY

Imagery can be described as images or mental pictures that have organized themselves into some kind of pattern. It makes some sense of the world for the person making images. He is very much like the artist in the act of creating the world the way he sees it: on the canvas of his mind appear images as he reacts to the world he sees and like the artist in the act of painting a picture, he gives organization and meaning to these images. How he depicts his world, what details he includes, the choices he makes of colors, the style he chooses, and the extent to which he allows his emotions to become involved are all dependent upon his emotional-intellectual make-up and the creative energizing forces at work at the time.

I have used analogy to explain imagery, which has been compared to a painting where a person's mind is the canvas on which is patterned his perceptions of the world. I may have just compared imagery to a painting and stopped there with no attempt to elaborate. Instead, I went on to add further details to the basic comparison where the individual is an artist and his mind the canvas, and by extending or elaborating the comparison, I have combined the images to make a more complex image pattern. To put it in another way "Imagery is like a painting" is a simple pattern whereas "Imagery is a painting on the canvas of Man's mind" is a complex image pattern. Simple and complex image patterns can be used in the act of comparison. The more highly imaginative among us tend to use more complex images. Whether we create personal, direct, symbolic, or fantasy analogies we use imagery. More often than not analogies with complex image patterns tend to be more interesting and provocative than simple image patterns as for instance, "John sings like a crow," when compared to "John sings like a featherless crow on a winter's day."

FIGURES OF SPEECH AS ANALOGY FORMS

In making analogies we may use any one of several well-known figures of speech based on agreement, similarity, or resemblance such as the similie, metaphor, personification, and allusion.

Similie

A simile is a form of comparison between two things that are different except in one particular characteristic to which you want to call attention like, "John is as *fat* as a pig," where John and pig are different in kind and yet possess one characteristic in common namely, being *fat*. By focusing attention on John's corpulence in this way we effectively describe *fat* John without lengthy description.

Metaphor

The metaphor is a condensed or implied simile. A comparison using this form attempts to relate two things differing in kind as if they were both similar or even identical, like saying "John is a pig." Here John is identified with the pig and with the implication that he does not only resemble the pig by being *fat* but also by possessing other pigish qualities. Thus by calling John a pig we are suggesting that John is not only fat but also *greedy*, *filthy*, *stinking*, and so on.

Personification

Personification is a form of comparison that attempts to give lifeless objects or abstract things attributes of life and feeling. One well-known example is "Time marches on," in which *Time* is given attributes of a human being moving forward on foot to indicate the steady passing of time. A variation of this, for instance: "With leaden foot Time creeps along," greatly slows down the pace while still retaining the inevitable forward movement.

Allusion

Allusion is another form of comparison which makes use of familiar phenomena in literature, mythology, legend, present day happenings, and so on. To explain or describe something without having to say much we can often relate this something to something else that is well known as for example the Biblical allusion: "She proved to be a good Samaritan," or the literary allusion: "David is the Falstaff of our company."

FIGURES OF SPEECH IN ANALOGIES

Each of the four figures of speech forms just described can be used as comparison forms in the four kinds of analogies. The *similie* "John is as fat as a pig," or the *metaphor* "John is a pig," are both *direct analogies*. As you know, if we wish to use the *simile* or *metaphor* in the form of *personal analogy* for instance, we will need to involve ourselves in the comparison like: "I'm fat as a pig," or "I'm a pig."

We can use *personification* in *personal analogy* and *direct analogy* as for instance: "I walked with death in Vietnam," or "Death took her for his bride."

Allusion may also be used in *personal analogy*. "I turned him to stone with my glassy stare," or "The bad news struck him down with the force of Jove's thunderbolt," are examples of *allusion* in the *direct analogy* form: the first allusion refers to the head of Medusa, and the second to the destructive energy of the king of the Greek gods.

When I discussed *symbolic analogy* I illustrated it by giving comparisons in the form of *simile* and *metaphor*. You will recall the "Rock" being used as the symbol of dependability, strength, stability, and consistency with the simile: "He is as firm as The Rock," and the *metaphor* "He is the Gibraltar of my life." If we wish to use the *allusion* of "cornerstone of our diplomacy in the Far East," we not only imply that he has the qualities of dependability, strength, stability and consistency, but also that he is the most important single building element upon which we expect to maintain the superstructure of our diplomacy.

We can go on to see that the same figures can be used to great effect in fantasy analogy. For instance, "jealousy" has been described in *Othello* as the "green-eyed monster." In simile form the comparison may read as, "His jealousy, like the green-eyed monster, will devour him," and in metaphor form, "Beware of jealousy, the green-eyed monster that destroys everything in its path."

Here are some exercises on analogies, imagery, and figures of speech which can be given to youths and adults:

Personal Analogy

Make a comparison which shows that you are involved in it. Say you are *thin* and you want others to know about it without having to give a lengthy description: a conventional example would be "I am as *thin* as a stick." This is a personal analogy with a simple image pattern. If you add details to it like "rotten in the middle" or "bent with use" you are adding further meaning to the basic image thus creating a complex image pattern.

Exercise 1 Construct a *personal analogy* with a simple image pattern that best describes say your body structure, head, or any other part of your anatomy. Try to think of a comparison object no one else would have thought of.

_____
_____

Exercise 2 Now add detail to make it into a complex image comparison.

_____
_____

Direct Analogy

Just as in personal analogy, a comparison in *direct analogy* form requires no self-involvement. To produce a direct analogy the "I" of the comparison above may become "he" or "Mary" to read "Mary, or he, is as thin as a stick."

Let us now try to find a comparison for *fat* in the direct analogy form. One such example could be: "John is as fat as a pig."

Exercise 1 Construct a *direct analogy* relative to *fat* using the *simple image* form.

_____
_____

Exercise 2 Now add detail to make it into a complex image comparison.

Symbolic Analogy

Let us say we come across someone who is dependable, strong, stable, consistent and so on, and we wish to convey this information effectively and without having to use too many words. We start by looking around for some phenomenon, animate or inanimate, which has as nearly as possible these qualities. The "Rock of Gibraltar" for example has been traditionally known to have such qualities. This "Rock" then can be used as "sign" or "symbol" of the qualities possessed by the person in mind. We may then refer to him using the symbolic analogy form as "He is the Gibraltar of my life" or "John is as firm as the Rock."

Exercise 1 Let us take another set of qualities like *life-giving*, *energizing*, and *beautiful*. Find one phenomenon for these characteristics and construct one *symbolic analogy* with *simple image structure*.

Exercise 2 Now add detail to make it into a *complex image* comparison.

Fantasy Analogy

In fantasy analogy the comparison object or subject at least must be imaginary. Myths, legends, allegories, fairy tales, and the like are all rich sources of imaginary materials for comparison, as for instance, the Devil, Medusa, Pandora's Box, Ariel, the Rainbow, the Dragon, the Garden of Eden, Paradise, Sugar Candy Mountain, Jekyll and Hyde, and so on.

Let us say that you wish to convey the information that someone you know is very wicked, evil, and murderous. You may compare such a person to Hyde using a simple image pattern like "John is Hyde himself" or using a complex image pattern like "Leonora's whispers stirred the Hyde in John."

Exercise 1 Construct a *fantasy analogy* with *simple image* pattern

_____
_____

Exercise 2 Now add detail to make it into a *complex image* comparison.

_____
_____

Figures and Analogies

1. Complete the following similes:
   (a) _____ as a needle.
   (b) Dead as a _____.
2. Make one *metaphor* for each of the following words:
   (a) Pillar _____.
   (b) Lightning _____.
3. Construct *personifications:*
   (a) Revenge _____.
   (b) Sorrow _____.
4. Find two *allusions* for:
   (a) Hope _____.
   (b) Light _____.

5. Using the above ideas construct one of each of the following:
   (a) Personal Analogy _____
   _____
   (b) Direct Analogy _____
   _____
   (c) Symbolic Analogy _____
   _____
   (d) Fantasy Analogy _____
   _____

6. Here is one word. Think about it for a while, then use your imagination to produce an analogy making it interesting and unusual, an analogy that others are not likely to think of:
   Green _____
   _____

   See if you can improve the quality and meaning of the analogy by adding detail to make the image more *complex:*
   _____
   _____
   _____

USING ANALOGY TO SOLVE PROBLEMS

There are at least three good approaches to solving problems creatively. One approach known as "Creative Problem Solving" sometimes associated with group brain-storming, and the most widely used method, was originated by Osborn (1948) and further developed by Parnes and other members of the Creative Education Foundation in the sixties and seventies. The problem-solving process of "Sociodrama" is another group creative problem-solving approach whose principles were first formulated by Moreno (1946) and later refined by him and others including Torrance (1975). Both approaches do not directly use analogy to help find solutions to problems. It is the "Synectics" approach to creative problem solving (Gordon, 1961; Prince, 1968) that uses analogy to help find solutions to problems.

Synectics attempts to teach a person the deliberate use of his creative resources. Prince (1968) has described it as "teaching an individual how to imitate, *whenever he desires*, the way he works on his 'on days'," thereby giving him the control of forcing new ideas and associations for conscious consideration rather than leaving him dependent on their chance occurrence.

When a person is faced with a problem he tries at first to understand the true nature of the problem or what Synectics terms as *making the strange familiar*. This is when he tries to find some relationship between the strangeness of the problem and what he already knows, an activity that involves analysis of the problem into component parts as preparation for the problem solver to find analogical relationships between them and familiar experiences and things. Gordon (1972) has described making the strange familiar as a "learning process" where understanding a problem or idea is done by bringing a *strange* concept into a *familiar* context. He gives the example of a student observing a fish's heart with no knowledge of physiology. His professor's explanation of how the heart works like a pump begins to make sense to the ignorant student only when he makes the learning connection between the heart and the water pump of a swimming pool where the dirty water is pumped through the filter and back into the pool. This also helps the student to understand how lungs and liver act as filters to cleanse the blood. By analogy, through the process of making the strange familiar, the student creatively contributes to his own learning.

Making the familiar strange is another important creative mechanism which Gordon calls the "innovation process" by which we consciously try to take a new look at the same old world, people, ideas, feelings, and things, just like "the child who in bending to look at the world from between his legs experiments with the familiar made strange." Gordon and his associates consider making the familiar strange the most important element in innovative problem solving because many breakthroughs have depended on looking at a *familiar* problem in a *strange* way. His example of Harvey's discovery of the heart's function in blood circulation very aptly illustrates this:

> ... in the 16th century, people thought that blood flowed from heart to body, surging in and out like the tides of the sea. Harvey was *familiar* with this view and believed it until he closely observed a fish's heart that was still beating after the fish had been opened up. Harvey looked for a tidal flow of blood, but the action of the fish's heart reminded him instead of a pump he had seen. The idea of the heart acting like a pump was most *strange* to him and he had to break his ebb and flow connection to make room for his new pump connection. Harvey's discovery, resulting from *making the familiar strange*, has saved countless lives by offering doctors an accurate account of the circulation of blood. (Gordon, 1972, p. 296).

ANALOGY AND CREATIVE WRITING

To the suggestions I had offered earlier in the chapter on using analogy in creative writing may be added an experimental creative writing course entitled *Making It Strange* developed by Gordon and associates (1968) for children in the intermediate grades. By helping students to learn the skills of making the familiar strange the authors encourage them to generate new ideas and help establish a mood for creative writing.

Another interesting set of materials is the *Imagi/Craft* materials developed by Cunnington and Torrance (1965) that also call attention to the value of using analogies in creative works. This is illustrated by dramatizations of how inventors use analogies to get their great ideas that lead to inventions, as for example the direct analogy of the human ear and the telephone used by Alexander Graham for making his invention. A good reading program by Clymer and Gates (1969) also gives students a variety of experiences in the use of analogy.

Students can also be encouraged to use analogy in their daily creative writing activities in school or at home in the informal writing activities that they may do by choice. One approach could be to have students write a paragraph or verse on a subject of interest following some warm-up activities relative to it. Then go over the writing to pick out factual presentation of the information for enrichment through analogies so that the writing becomes full and vital, and what once was black and white is now in color.

In the same way, the quality of children's speech can be improved. Create a situation for a short conversation and record it. Then play back the conversation for the students to listen. Ask them to figure out more interesting ways to express what they had spoken and encourage them to play about with and speak in analogies. This kind of activity can not only lead to exciting modes of speech but also prepare the way for effective dramatization of events and stories that may eventually lead to the writing of simple but powerful little plays.

These are but a few ways you can use analogies to enrich your child's thinking, writing, and speaking. I am sure you can think of many other ways of applying the different approaches suggested in this chapter to stir your child's imagination to be creative. Remember you are working with one of the most potent creative energy sources. The person who has learned not only to think in analogies but also deliberately use it as needed stands an excellent chance of being creative, inventive, and a good problem solver.

6: Some Problems of Creatively Gifted Children

Along with the attention we have given to measurement and some of the ways we can encourage your child to think in creative ways, must come an awareness of some of the special problems highly gifted children experience as they grow up.

Remember what I said earlier in the book about Lewis Terman, the man who constructed the Stanford Binet. Terman was also a serious student of highly gifted children. His research on the *Genetic Studies of Genius* (1959) and that of Oden (1968) in two follow-up studies over periods of 35 and 40 years respectively, reported that the geniuses studied had grown to be gifted adults who maintained their intellectual ability, had lower mortality rates, good physical and mental health, manifested minimal crime, ranked high in educational and vocational achievements, were active in community affairs, and held moderate political and social views, and with two-thirds of them feeling that they had realized their potential. Another study (Cox, 1969) concluded that geniuses are not only characterized in childhood by superior I.Q. but also by traits of interest, energy, will, and character that foreshadow later performance.

Oden (1968) in attempting to assess the relationships of vocational achievement and genius, compared 100 most and least successful male geniuses and found that the most successful men came from families having higher socio-economic status and giving more encouragement to succeed. They also ranked higher as adolescents in volitional, intellectual, moral and social traits, and had more self-confidence, perseverance, and integration toward goals. In addition, although scholastic achievement had been similar in grade school, half as many of the least successful men had graduated from college. They were also found to be more prone to emotional and social difficulties.

Not many of us know that when children give trouble the reason for this may be because they are highly gifted. Many of the problems of such children stem from the conflicts they have with the people around them, between the single person, several people or the people's representatives in education, government, social organizations, and so on.

The gifted child is often dominated by the inner forces of his creativity that make him do things sometimes beyond his control. They may require him to be independent and nonconforming in his relations with others, who may insist that he do what they have planned for him and in their way. This often leads to conflicts and confrontations that constantly call for the child's adjustment. He may either learn to cope with the rising tensions, or he may repress his creative needs. If he is able to deal with these difficulties then they will lead him to productive behavior and mental health. If he is unable to deal with these difficulties and represses them, then they will lead to many personality problems and possible breakdown or mental ill-health.

Torrance (1962) describes the problems of the highly creative child who as a "minority of one" must learn to cope with the sanctions of society against his divergency; he must learn to express his talents without alienating his friends; he must cope with the demands of our system to be well-rounded to the extent of giving up productive ways of expressing himself to do what he is most interested in and best able to do rather than to do what is expected of him because he is a boy or a girl; he needs to learn in his own way rather than in ways prescribed by others; he has to continue to attempt the difficult and test the limits in risk-taking behavior in spite of discouragement and control, and to find direction and purpose in what he is doing.

Further, Torrance considers that we need to recognize that the creative child has a set of values that may be quite different from the group to which he belongs, so that we may help the child to maintain his creativity without being obnoxious. He would also have us know that the creative child is the kind of person who often cannot stop working because his creative energies do not allow him to stop thinking especially in relation to productive work.

ADJUSTMENT OF CREATIVE CHILDREN

From Frank Barron (1963) we learn that a creative person is one who prefers complexity, tolerates imbalance, disorder, ambiguity, and incompleteness. Such a person often plays about with the irrational in himself because he sees in it the source of much of his original thinking.

Barron also tells us that the creative person rejects the demands of society's claim that everyone should adapt themselves to a norm for a given time and place: the rebellion, refusal to adjust and adamant insistence on the importance of the self and of individuality is often the mark of a healthy character.

He also points out that the creative person is also virtuous in the simple moral sense of the term:

> Psychologically healthy people do what they think is right, and what they think is right is that people should not lie to one another or to themselves, that they should not steal, slander, persecute, intrude, do damage

willfully, go back on their word, fail a friend, or do any of the things that put them on the side of death as against life (Barron, 1968, p. 145).

A person who is mentally healthy can productively cope with his problems that may come up between himself and others; he knows how to resolve the conflict between maintaining his independence and conforming to society's needs so that he can be productive. Some of the strategies he uses have been described by Pauline Pepinsky (1960) as follows:

he translates his own ideas into language relevant to others so that they can see his contribution as instrumental to (or as in minimal conflict with) their own needs;
he states his criticism in a positive and constructive way;
he makes it evident that basically he stands for something that commands the respect of others in the group;
he minimizes personal threat to others by granting them dignity; he will listen;
he builds up a "credit rating" and "buys" more freedom over a period of time by initial service in terms of existing demands and requirements;
he focuses upon the job to be done, not on "personalities," nor on acquiring status as an end in itself; and
he takes into account matters of timing; he is able to delay response as well as to act.

Common to all these adjustment problems of the highly creative child and of central relevance is his psychological isolation and estrangement from peers, teachers, and parents since his propensity to be nonconforming, independent, and productive in his thinking create tensions between himself and others leading to the application of pressure tactics of one kind or another to bring him in line.

The highly creative child may find ways and means to remain both productive and socially acceptable as has been suggested by Pauline Pepinsky and others; however, if he is not able to then we must step in to help him acquire those skills and strategies that will allow him to accomplish this. Otherwise he may repress his creativity, and while appearing to conform, is probably having internal conflicts that will lead him to require counseling or therapy.

PROBLEMS OF REPRESSING CREATIVE NEEDS

Repression of his creative needs may lead the highly creative child to become outwardly conforming, obedient, and dependent, with damaging consequences to his concept of self. It may also lead to serious learning disabilities and behavioral problems. In preferring to learn by authority he sacrifices his natural tendency to learn creatively by questioning, guessing, exploring, and experimenting. As a result he loses interest in and is resistant to learning. Development of awe for masterpieces and a spread of feelings of inadequacy from deficiency in one area of learning to other areas of learning where no deficiency exists follow. Further, much of the aggressive behaviors in the classroom that the highly gifted child exhibits can be traced to his inability to use creative and scientific thinking strategies to overcome his tensions. These tensions often arise from his reactions to a school curriculum that is unchallenging, repetitive, reproductive, and boring, before they become problems that result in his misbehavior.

The more serious problem of prolonged enforced repression of the creative child's needs may lead to emotional problems and neurosis, and even psychosis (for example, Gowan, 1955; Torrance, 1962). Neurosis as you know is a condition generated by acute and prolonged anxiety states and can be very much the case of continued repression of creative needs especially in the context of conflict situations. Neurosis hinders rather than facilitates the functioning of the creative process contrary to popular opinion. Kubie (1958) writing about this subject suggests that many a creative man of the arts and sciences refuses therapy because he erroneously believes that his "creative zeal and spark" is dependent upon his neurosis; what is really essential is that the preconscious process functions freely to gather, assemble, compare and reshuffle ideas in the activity of creation.

Torrance (1962) writes of psychosis relative to maladjustment of the creative individual in a special sense. In psychosis resulting from the blocking of creative energies, thinking is often paralyzed and the imagination functions in a way that cannot distinguish between reality and irreality. The creative individual who has his productivity blocked may develop behavior traits similar to those of psychotics:

> ... his reaction to reality may be very much like the behavior of the paranoid personality. For example, a highly creative individual, because of the very superiority of his thinking and production may be threatening to others. In actuality he may experience a great deal of persecution. His reaction of this reality may be very much like the behavior of the paranoid personality in some respects. Or in order to accomplish significant creative work, an individual may have to behave in ways which are judged as withdrawn or schizophrenic (p. 136).

These conditions no longer bespeak of the thin partitions that divide the two regions of genius and madness about which Alexander Pope poeticized. In psychosis they become indistinguishable. The distinctive feature of the mentally healthy creator, as it were, is his ability to cross over the boundary momentarily, at will, in the act of creation, with controls to return from fantasy to reality.

Another problem of the highly creative child is to be found in circumstances of deprivation. The children who come from poorer home environments are at a disadvantage: not only do they lack material things but also intellectual stimulation. Besides, they may be hindered as well from acquiring adequate verbal concepts and communication skills to handle the mental operations which are usually demanded on traditional measures of intelligence with consequent misinterpretations of the child's potential so that he is erroneously labelled as mentally retarded and treated as such. Many of the other problems already described, like behavioral disorders, faulty concept of self, and learning disabilities are also pertinent to the highly creative but socioeconomically disadvantaged child.

PARENT AND TEACHER AS COUNSELOR

In a counseling situation the conditions fostering creativity include *psychological safety* wherein acceptance of the child's worth is unconditional and where there is absence of external evaluation and presence of emphatic understanding; and *psychological freedom* wherein the child can feel completely free, and can express himself and feel fully the experience of the moment (Rogers, 1954).

As counselor Torrance tells us we can explore the highly creative child's problems and assist him to find ways and means to overcome them (1962). You may bear in mind, while you are thus involved, of the effects of positive reward and reinforcement, the child's possession of many talents, and the need to recognize when his divergency is the product of mental health, illness or delinquency; you can assist him by reducing overemphasis on sex roles so that he may be able to accept his softness and femininity as well as his intellectual autonomy; you can help him maintain his creative positives while not being obnoxious about his expression; you can reduce his feelings of isolation by teaching him to tolerate his separateness, estranged from his teachers and peers; you can help him cope with his anxieties and irrational fears; you can teach him how to deal with hardships and failure towards more constructive activities of exploration, experimentation and project initiation, in an atmosphere of freedom from penalty that at one and the same time places great value on high standards. Your increased sensitivity to the creative child's needs and problems will help you to differentiate the fuzzy mess you are confronted with at the outset of the counseling relation from the true nature of the problem to render the highly creative child appropriate assistance and direction.

SOME WAYS TO PREVENT THESE PROBLEMS

A few years ago John Gowan gave us some useful clues about what we can do to help creatively gifted children to maintain mental health and productivity (Gowan and Torrance, 1971). Among the many valuable suggestions he offers us, the ones that relate most to what we can do to help prevent some of the problems experienced by the creative child are providing a fostering attitude, facilitating the child's own mental health, facilitating the creative child's social relationships, and facilitating peer friendships.

1. *On Providing a Fostering Attitude* he suggests that we should:
    avoid setting up unfavorable evaluation of the child's attempts to create, instead he tells us to be supportive of the child's ability to create, and to be sympathetic to his first failures;

- provide a warm and safe psychological base from which to explore, and to which the child may return when he is frightened by his own discoveries;
- be tolerant of new ideas, be respectful of their curiosity and questioning and ideas, seek to answer their questions even though they may seem to be too wild; and
- let the child be alone and carry out things on his own if he wishes, for too much supervision can hinder this productivity.

2. *On Facilitating The Child's Own Mental Health* he suggests that we:
   - help the child to learn how to build his own value system and not necessarily rely on his own, so that he will know how to value himself, his ideas and others, and their ideas, and be in turn appropriately values;
   - help take care of his needs according to Maslow's hierarchy of needs (that is, body needs, safety, love, esteem of self and others) so that he can be ready to become the person who fulfils himself (that is, realizes cognitive actualization), for a person who worries about the basic needs and about what others, and their ideas, and be in turn appropriately valued;
   - help him handle disappointments and doubts when he stands alone in some creative act which his fellows do not understand so that he will maintain his creativity finding reward within himself for being creative and not worry too much for the approval of others which, though slow in coming, will eventually come;
   - help him understand that these are areas of his life where there is more than one answer to a question, and other areas where there are no answers because the question is not well asked, so that he can learn

to live with this kind of intellectual tension without aborting the ideas that produce it;

help the child value himself as a creative person while having to show disapproval for some of his behavior that is not socially acceptable;

help him to learn how to lean far enough into himself (that is, preconscious) to capture floating ideas, and give sympathy rather than disapproval to his early and crude attempts to make these ideas socially acceptable; and

help him by praising his new-born creative efforts, avoid criticizing his initial creativity however crude it may be, and do this in an air of sympathetic expectancy, attitude of warmth and even affection, for the child tends to create for those he loves.

3. *On Facilitating the Creative Child's Social Relations* he suggests that we need to help the child:

become a "reasonable adventurer" and to take reasonable cognitive visits or intuitive leaps, for by so doing such a person is most likely to hit upon a real discovery or breakthrough;

maintain the essentials of his creativity while at the same time helping them to avoid public disapproval, to reduce socially caused tensions, and to cope with peer sanctions;

become constructively creative by giving him more responsibility when we find him nonconstructively creative;

become a constructive rather than nonconstructive nonconformist, for if we think of the child's mind as a twin volcano of creativeness and destructiveness, the more we open the creative one the more we tend to close the destructive one—since the child who is denied constructive cognitive creative outlets may turn to become creatively devious.

4. *On Facilitating Peer Friendships* he describes the prob-

lem and suggests what parents can do about it as follows:

Gifted children, especially young ones, often have difficulty in making friends (psychologists say he gets into the peer state) at about the age of seven. At this time there is a marked withdrawal from the family and the child finds someone just like himself, same age, same sex, same clothes, same breakfast food, same TV shows with whom to identify. Parents often think the child has fallen under the evil influence of the neighbor's child and the neighbor thinks the same thing. Despite parental anguish the child is learning a most important lesson—how to identify with others. It is terribly important to be able to get along with and be liked by other members of your own sex, and this is the time when boys learn to be *regular fellers* and girls learn the same lesson.

But if he is a gifted child, one in a hundred, he has to know 100 other boys to find one like himself, and half the time the hundredth child is a girl, and he's sunk. It does no good to tell the child at this stage that the world is made up of all kinds of people, and he must like them all. He starts in by identifying with someone like himself. Many gifted children develop imaginary playmates to fill the void left by not having true peers. Education should allow for cluster grouping in the elementary grades, and parents should bus children around after school to find others they can play with. A gifted child with a chronological age of 8 and a mental age of 11 can't be expected to play with average children of either age—he won't get along with his age peers and average children aged 11 won't admit him to their games. He needs to find another child who is 8 but thinks like 11. This may take some parental doing but it's much better than letting the child develop lonely antisocial habits because no one else seems to be like him. So when a child becomes so absorbed in his own activities that he doesn't have friends, it's because he hasn't had a chance to make the right kind (Gowan and Torrance, 1971, pp. 185-186).

7: Creative Development of the Child

Another thing about the creatively gifted child that should catch our interest is his creativity and productivity as it relates to age. That is to say, were there any particular times of his life when he was more creative than at other times; or does his creativity show increase as he grows older? This means that we need to find out if his creative development takes place in discrete stages or is continuous.

Two major thoughts on this matter come from Gowan and Torrance. While Gowan tends to think about creative development as something that relates to definite periods of a person's life (1971), Torrance tends to see it as an ongoing process of development that should manifest itself as the child grows older (1968).

STAGES OF CREATIVE DEVELOPMENT

Gowan tells us that though we may regard creative development like growth, to be continuous, so that as we grow up our creativity grows up as well, this is not likely to happen. He thinks creative development occurs in stages and finds support for this theory in what Freud, Erickson, and Piaget have said about development.

Development for each of these three men takes place in

stages though each one has different names for them and thinks about each stage in a different way. Freud's five affective developmental stages, he says, fits rather neatly the chronological stages of Piaget's five cognitive stages. To Freud's final stage of development Erickson has added four more stages, and Gowan wonders if at a future date some other theorist may not find a matching four more cognitive stages though if these stages do not match we should not be unhappy.

The Latency Period (Stages 1, 4, and 7)

For the infant (0-1), this is the period when he gets to know the things around him, to experience the thing character of the world. As a youth (7-12) he begins to know things for their size, shape, form, and color and what one makes out of them. As an adult (26-40) he is concerned with others who are important to him such as children, their productions, art creations, and other "mental children."

Common to the infant, youth, and adult is his immersion in the world of senses. Things get done, changes occur, no self-consciousness is felt, very little time is left to assess feelings or to be concerned with the questions of "Who am I?" Accomplishments strengthen and prepare the person to search for his identity.

Identity (Stages, 2, 5 and 8)

The infant, youth, and adult are concerned here with questions like "Who am I? Why do I exist? How am I in relation to others? What happens to me when I die? Will I be saved?" During these times the person searches within himself for answers, withdraws rather than returns, defies authority rather than obeys it, and "marches to the music of a different drum." At each stage, he tries to come to terms with himself: as an infant he searches for his identity, as a youth he redefines it in terms of what he can do, and as an adult he again redefines it in terms of the meaning of his life and death in the cosmos.

Others find it difficult to live with an individual passing through these stages—the infant with his negativism, and adolescent with his idealism, demand for independence and rebellion against authority both by his attitudes and actions. During this time of turning into himself and away from the world it is easy for him to believe that no one understands him, often spending too much time in self-examination, forgetting the real world outside himself leading to moodiness resulting from the discrepancy between what he wants to be and what he finds he can be and do.

Creativity (Stages 3, 6 and 9)

During stages 3 and 6, which deal with love, the person passes from love of self through love of parent of the opposite sex to generalized love of people of both sexes and to love of one person of the opposite sex. Stage 9 may very well exist where love is for all mankind given in the way of Buddah and Christ (Agape-Love).

Gowan sees love as required for creation both physically and mentally. That is why stages 3 and 6 are important: creativity first develops during stage 3 when a person gains control of his environment through affectional relations with the parent of the opposite sex such that "boys" who are affectionately close to their mothers and "girls" who are unusually close to their fathers, during 4 to 7 years, tend to become more creative than others of similar ability. It is during this period that warm affection given by the opposite-sex parent freely enlarges the bridge between the fantasy life and real world of the child.

Again in stage 6, adolescent creativity is normally enhanced through the inspiration of loving and being loved by a person of the opposite sex; however, in some cases of adolescent love, consummation involving physical relations tends to reduce the high energy potential aroused, but when delayed or partly prevented from being used, great art, music and literature result.

Love in our lives is seen as central to creativity so that if we want to be creative we should put more love into our lives. Although the developmental process of stages 3 and 6 naturally emphasize creativity, it is not completely absent at the other stages of development. Love and creativity may enter into our lives environmentally at any time and the degree to which love is abundant is the degree to which creativity is likely to be present. However, a good start in stage 3 is expected to give the best assurance that creativity will occur again in stage 6. Gowan says:

> One becomes creative as a by-product of the beloved. One strives to please, and in pleasing the loved one, pulls things out of the preconscious that one hardly knew was there. Or alternatively, because one's mental health is improved, one finds the preconscious teeming with treasure to share with the beloved, and these goodies often bubble forth without conscious effort (1971, pp. 162-163).

The term preconscious originated with Freud who divided the mental life of the psyche of a person into unconscious, preconscious and conscious. This is very simply explained by Sullivan (1953, p. 161) as the "bad-me," "not-me," "good-me." "Bad-me," or the unconscious, refers to that part of our mental life that stores ideas and drives that cause too much pain, anxiety or guilt to us if we are conscious or aware of them; and we do this to defend the self (ego) by pushing them aside (repression) and in other ways. Of course these ideas and drives remain active in our unconscious and without our awareness are the cause of some of our behaviors. Sometimes we notice them when our defenses are relaxed as in dreams, in slips of the tongue, or when we are under the influence of alcohol or drugs. "Good-me" is that part of our mental life of which we are aware which can be called the "conscious positive self-concept." "Not-me" is the part of our mental life where frightening and uncanny experiences occur like those we meet in dreams and nightmares. It is the preconscious or "not-me" area of our mental life that is the source of much of our creativity (Gowan, 1974, p. 81).

In a series of analogies Gowan (1975) explains that the preconscious can be considered:

> ... as an ever-refilling well wherein all creative men have learned to dip their bucket, or as a great general computer, containing in its data banks all knowledge, and creativity is but the process of operating the terminal console. Or it can be considered as a great collator, chewing up the events and ideas of the day, and rearranging them into other forms and patterns, or like an enlarged fluid container, with a permeable membrane through which (by osmosis) creative ideas are leaked into consciousness (p. 301).

He has illustrated this last analogy where the preconscious is compared to an enlarged fluid container through whose permeable membrane creative ideas leak into the consciousness as follows (1974, p. 83).

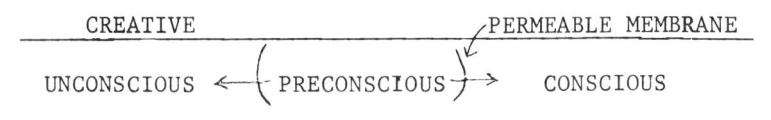

```
CREATIVE                            PERMEABLE MEMBRANE
                       
   UNCONSCIOUS  ←—( PRECONSCIOUS )—→   CONSCIOUS
```

Gowan also tells us that the preconscious is the source of man's creativity especially if it is strengthened, protected and enlarged through regular use and through increased mental health. At first the creative person makes use of his preconscious intuitively, when leaks occur through the permeable

GOWAN'S PERIODIC TABLE OF DEVELOPMENTAL STAGES

	LATENCY (The World: it, they)	IDENTITY (The Ego: I, me)	CREATIVITY (The Other: thou)
INFANT	1. Thing oriented Sexually latent relative to individual with his world of experience World of percepts (0-1)	2. All about "me" Finds his identity Negativism (2-3)	3. Deal with love relations Expansion from self-love to love of parents (4-6)
YOUTH	4. Size, shape, form and color of things and what one can make out of them (7-12)	5. Redefines his identity in terms of what he can do as a young adult Clamor for independence Idealism Attitude and action anathema to authority figure (13-17)	6. Generalized heterosexual love to love one person of opposite sex (18-25)
ADULT	7. World of significant others such as child Broaden to world of ideas, formulas, production, art creations and other mental children (26-40)	8. Again redefines his identity in terms of meaning of his life and death in the (40-onward)	9. Love all mankind (Buddah-Christ type)

membrane, as it were by osmosis, and manifests itself in works of art of one kind or another. At a higher level of creativity (psychedelia or state of mind expansion that takes place naturally and not with the help of drugs), the barriers that separate the preconscious from the unconscious and conscious are thought of as doors that swing open to let in, as it were, the resources of the preconscious for cognitive processing and production (1974, p. 83).

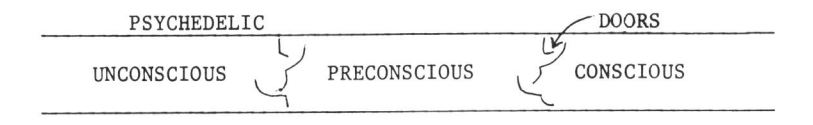

PSYCHEDELIC		DOORS
UNCONSCIOUS	PRECONSCIOUS	CONSCIOUS

If the preconscious becomes open in this way to a person then he becomes creative, and he explains this in terms of the printing of a new edition of old newspapers. He compares the preconscious to an editor who obtains the material he needs for this new edition from the archives of the unconscious which contain all his past experiences, in chewed-up and digested form—a vast assortment of biological impulses, tabooed acts, rejected compromises, affected pains and pleasures, remembered facts, personal feelings, horrifying nightmares and a host of other material. What the new edition is to be will depend upon the extent to which the editor finds the unconscious accessible (1975, p. 301).

Where stage 6 in the periodic table (presented earlier in the chapter) stresses creative forces at work, it is an intuitive kind of creativity that prepares a person for psychedelic creativity of stage 7 when the resources of the preconscious become available not so much by chance but almost at will.

Gowan asks us to observe an important happening in nature and in human life which he relates to a "transformation of energy" that takes place from one stage of development to the next higher stage of development. This he calls *periodicity*, which "occurs when the same pattern of events is seen to run through higher development as has been contained in a corresponding pattern from a lower sequence"—something that seems to have escaped the notice of human development theorists.

For instance, common and important to the developmental stages of Freud, Erickson and Piaget is the concept of periodicity or periodic rhythm. Gowan says that our lives can be divided into three major periods, the infant (0-6 years), youth (7-25 years), and adult (26-40 years). During each of these three periods, we tend to pass through three stages, namely, latency, identity and creativity; and each time these occur at a higher level. A simplified version of Gowan's periodic table of developmental stages follows.

DEVELOPMENT AS CONTINUOUS

Torrance tells us that he and his associates have found that discontinuities, at least in the dominant culture of the United States, were even more severe for creative thinking abilities than for other kinds of mental development. Certain clear periods of decline in creative thinking abilities were found to occur especially for children at about ages 5, 9, 13, and 17. The worst occurred at about age 9 or the fourth grade—what he has called the fourth grade slump in creative thinking abilities—at which time the greatest amount of personality disturbance, behavior problems, learning difficulties, and the like were noticeable.

He checked this by studying 100 children over a period of more than four years (September, 1959 to May, 1964) and found that on the average, slumps in the four creative thinking abilities (fluency, flexibility, originality, and elaboration) did occur at the fourth grade level; for while 45 to 61 percent of the children showed drops there were a few who showed increases in creative thinking abilities. Generally he found that children tended to improve in the fifth grade though many of them scored lower than they did in the third grade on the tests he gave them.

He then explored (Torrance, 1967) if children in other cultures would also be affected in the same way and found that:

> ... cultural factors strongly influence the course of creative development, the level of creative functioning, and the type of creative functioning that flourishes most. In some cultures, development is relatively continuous. In others, there is little growth during the elementary school years. In most, however, there are discontinuities. In general, these discontinuities occur at about the beginning of the fourth grade or the end of the third grade; in some groups, discontinuities do not appear until the sixth grade. There are a number of indications that these discontinuities occur within a culture whenever children in that culture are confronted with new stresses and demands. When Christian missions and similar groups establish schools in underdeveloped areas, they apparently bring both a stimulating and disrupting influence on development, producing discontinuities in creative development (p. 301).

Study of the problem in terms of the production of original verbal images (Khatena, 1971c, Khatena and Fisher, 1974) showed drops in children's originality as occurring especially in the upper elementary grades (grades 4 to 6) or between the ages of 9 to 11 years. When this was checked by studying a group of the same children over a period of 4 years, it was found that loss in originality did occur in children between the ages of 9 and 10 years or at about the fourth grade level with some gain showing at the age of 11 years. These findings lend further support to Torrance's observations concerning the fourth grade slump in creative thinking abilities.

RELATIONSHIP BETWEEN THE TWO APPROACHES

It is interesting to note that for Gowan and Torrance, the preschool years of the child (4 to 6 years) are creative times. The child's entry into stage 4 of the next periodic rhythm (7 to 12 years) brings about a change of focus from control of the environment through his affectional relationships with the parent of the opposite sex, in stage 3, which enhances his creativity, to that of the world and his increased attempt to understand it for what it is which reduces his creative potential. These changes seem to coincide with the child's entry into elementary school where the real world is emphasized, where pressures become more formally exercised by one of the most powerful agents of society, where conformity and correct behavior are emphasized, and where restrictions of more natural ways of learning are established—a period observed by Torrance as generally showing little growth in creative thinking abilities, and the first and most severe of the slumps in creative development.

However, stage 4 (7 to 12 years) is not a period of high creative potential with decrement in creativity as occurring between the ages of 9 and 10 years. So what we have is a period of relatively low creative potential at which time the child experiences all kinds of school pressures and retarding influences. Those few who are able to adjust and adapt to them, tend not to show the loss in creative thinking abilities that most of the others show at this time. And those who recover from the loss experienced at about the fourth grade level, in the fifth grade do not surpass their achievement shown in grade 3.

COUNTERACTING MEASURES

We have been in search for ways and means to overcome the problem of decrements in creativity especially at a time when children seem to be very vulnerable, and Torrance and others have shown conclusively that by arranging proper stimulating conditions and opportunities for creative achievement that much can be done to prevent the fourth grade slump. Gowan has added the dimension of love which tends to prepare and predispose the person for creative thoughts and acts, and for appropriate links that may be established between the conscious and preconscious so that the ability to dip into the preconscious to bring back creative ideas at will is developed. In Chapter Five I have suggested some ways you can encourage and stimulate your children's creativity and imagination.

It would be very useful to help your child to be creative during the ages of 4 and 6 or stage 3, especially if you observe that he shows signs of being low in his ability to be creative. You might also give him many opportunities to be creative around the ages of 9 and 10 years which is within stage 4 of the Gowan developmental model (7-12 years). Of course you will have to be on the lookout for the times when he is exposed to much stress, and over long periods of time; so do what you can to take some of it away. Entry points into various levels of schooling do expose your child to stress and you should be particularly watchful over the pressures brought to bear upon him by his new surroundings, teachers, friends and learning. With your understanding and help he may avoid this difficult period of his life, or overcome these pressures while continuing to maintain his creativity and be productive.

8: Parent and Teacher Hold the Key

If you think you have a gifted child do not be afraid to talk about it. You may find out that there are others like you. If your child does well on one kind of test of giftedness but not on another, do not be alarmed. There are many ways a child can be gifted.

A gifted child, who is not challenged by his school work, becomes quickly bored and even troublesome: he may lose interest in the work given to him—school assignments and learning that are really planned for average kids. As a teacher, be watchful of this and plan educational experiences that will make his learning a living thing, an adventure into the unknown where you can sometimes join him as a fellow explorer. As a parent, be sensitive for such clues and arrange to meet the child's teacher. Sometimes an understanding talk will do so much to enrich the child's school life in a way that will prevent the occurrence of many problems.

If we are not alert to the needs of creatively gifted children we may help them to lose or give up this very precious energy in their lives. Sometimes the creatively gifted child will find ways to be successful in spite of the negative influences and restrictions in their lives, the misery of being misunderstood and the punishment that follows. You can help the gifted child by reducing the "No's" in his life at home and in school. Each time you do not want him to do something, and often it is for his own good, help him understand this, and provide him with, or better still, encourage him to discover alternative behavior. Take away the drudgery of busy work; help liven up his learning; make him want to learn, encourage him to set goals to be achieved; involve him fully in the learning experience so that he learns with thinking abilities and feelings; and allow him the freedom to learn in creative ways: such practice will remove the acute tensions and conflicts that hurt him because of his extraordinary sensitivity.

Be alert to signs of his creative potential blossoming and help him to effect the transformation. You can do much by just standing aside and letting the creatively gifted child become and grow. We sometimes smother him with too much of what we think is best for him. Feel privileged to watch the caterpillar turn into a butterfly: it is not often that you can be witness to the transformation, and understand that just because you did not interfere it happened naturally.

Affection plays such a great part in the creative act, and the closeness and nurture of caring will bring to fruit productions that would otherwise never take place. The energy of affectionate relations between child and parent of the opposite sex also may operate between child and teacher. Be aware of this since children will create for whom they care. You do have considerable power to facilitate productivity, and if you will take the trouble to act in a nurturant way to accept him fully and to be his support when he needs you, creativity will flourish before you as if by magic, and the thrill of the good fairy or magician is yours.

A child is usually regarded as gifted if he has an I.Q. of 132 and above by many people. But we know today that this is one important way to know if a child is gifted. If you have a child who is bright normal or has an I.Q. of between 115 to about 125 you might arrange to have him tested for creative thinking abilities as well. It will then give you a better picture of his abilities. This you can do by taking him to a psychologist who can have access to tests of creative thinking abilities which you will not have. The information he will be able to give you of your child can be very valuable. It may be that your child is smart in nonverbal ways, so when you have your child screened make sure to request that he be given tests that tell you if he is verbally or nonverbally gifted, or gifted in both ways.

As you know a person may be gifted in a number of different ways. You can find this out by talking to the psychologist who can, by examining how your child has done on parts of a test, tell you what his strong and weak abilities are. Sometimes he may have to use more than one test to find out this information which can be more important to know than just the child's I.Q. In this way you can find out, for instance, what abilities he tends to use more often than others, and which of them can be put to work for better performance. In this respect Guilford's model of the intellect as a center for processing different kinds of information has encouraged the production, for instance, of a series of books on developing the five intellectual processing capacities, namely, cognition, memory, convergent thinking, divergent thinking and evaluation (Meeker and Sexton, n.d.).

The best of the individual I.Q. tests are the Stanford Binet and the Wechsler Scales of Intelligence for Children. Of course there are group I.Q. tests, and these have been mentioned in Chapter Two. It is preferable to have your child screened for I.Q. by one of the individual measures. However, it may not always be possible. If your child is screened by a group test and there is reason to doubt the findings check this out by arranging that your child be given either the Binet or Wechsler Scale. However, obtaining your child's I.Q. is not enough. You should also see to it that your child is screened for creative thinking abilities as well. Guilford's *Creativity Tests for Children*, the *Torrance Tests of Creative Thinking*, and *Thinking Creatively with Sounds and Words* may be used for the purpose. The combined information so derived will help you get a clearer picture of how gifted your child is and in what areas.

While you may have to rely on the help of a psychologist to formally determine that your child is creatively gifted you can also screen your child using a measure which will not require any special training. One such instrument is a creativity checklist or inventory called *Something About Myself*: it is an instrument designed in a way that teachers and parents can use. Another companion instrument is *What Kind of Person Are You?* Both are published as the *Khatena-Torrance Creative Perception Inventory*, and are suitable for identifying children who are creatively gifted 12 years and up when children are required to write their own responses.

Something About Myself has also been successfully tried with children who were 10 and 11 years old as well but with adult help. If the measure is to be used with younger children, then an adult must observe the child and respond to the items of the inventory for the child. The instrument has not as yet been used with children below the age of 10 and may not be suitable for purposes of identifying very young creatively gifted children.

How *Something About Myself* can be used by you to identify your creative child has been described in Chapter Four. Quite simply, administer the test according to the instructions given in the Directions Manual. You can then find out how creative he perceives himself to be by just a straight count of his positive responses: the higher the score obtained the more creative he is according to the scale. The measure also groups the items into six creative orientations, namely, Environmental Sensitivity, Initiative, Self Strength, Intellectuality, Individuality, and Artistry. A very highly creative child will tend to be high on all six creative orientations. But generally I have found that the child is low on Initiative, and to some extent below average on Artistry.

Once you have determined his scores on the total scale and the six creative orientations you will have identified not only how creative he is but his strengths and weaknesses on the scale. Your next step would be to plan experiences that will help encourage the use of those creative characteristics in which he is weak. I have given an example of this in Chapter Four. In Chapter Five there are other examples as well. *Ideabooks* (Myers and Torrance, 1964/1966), *New Directions in Creativity* (Renzulli, 1973), *Classroom Ideas for Encouraging Thinking and Feeling* (Williams, 1970), and *Structure of Intellect Abilities Workbook on Divergent Thinking* (Meeker and Sexton, n.d.), provide many useful exercises as well. You can also find information about other useful materials relative to creative thinking and problem solving in a book by Feldhusen and Treffinger (1977).

Some of the exercises will have to be developed by you relative to the characteristics of the measure. With a bit of imagination and effort you can have a fine thing going for your child at home and in the classroom. The important thing is that this puts you in the driver's seat, and you can go places with your children in developing the use of their creative qualities.

It is very important that you pay attention to your child's use of analogy and imagery, both of which are very closely related to the creative imagination at work. You can encourage your child to think in ways that break old habits of thought, to use the thinking process that will allow them to pull apart things organized in one way so that he may rearrange the parts in fresh and novel combinations, and to process information in many different and new combinations. You may plan experiences for him that call for the use of analogy and figures of speech all of which have been described, and with some exercises that you can use, modify and extend for your own needs.

I have found that children tend to use the direct analogy form most of all, and that they need practice in the use of personal analogy and fantasy analogy as well. The use of symbolic analogy is dependent on the child's intellectual maturity and can be delayed until the child is in high school. I have also found that the child tends to use simple images rather than complex images when he is in the upper elementary grades, and that as he grows older he tends to use more complex images. One of the things you can do would be to assist him in learning how to add meaningful details to the simple images he produces. How you can do this has also been suggested in Chapter Five.

You will find your gifted child generally a healthy person both in mind and body, able to get along rather well with others, and does well in school. However, if he is continually restricted in his development and learning you may find him becoming increasingly troublesome. You can help by freeing him from some of the restrictions that do not allow him to grow, and help him to achieve independence and be himself.

Restrictions cause tensions and conflicts, and over long periods of time may lead to the child's mental ill-health. You cannot really remove all the obstructions in his life but you can help him learn to cope with them. Teach him to recognize that there are many alternatives to the solution of a problem, that he may have to know as much as he can about a problem before he can begin to handle it, that he may need to think of many ideas that could be used to solve the problem and write them down, that he will have need to judge the best idea for the solution and he can do this by deciding what is required for a good solution—in short he needs to know about the creative problem solving process and taught to use it. In this respect, you will find *Guide to Creative Action* and *Creative Actionbook* (Parnes, Noller & Biondi, 1977ab) to be very useful. Thinking by analogy may also be helpful, and if your child understands how to use this mechanism he may find that solutions to problems come to him more easily.

Many suggestions about what you can do to help him overcome and even prevent problems have been outlined in Chapter Six. Briefly, they tell you not to overemphasize what the child must do because of being a boy or a girl; to help him continue to be productive without being obnoxious about it; to help him understand why sometimes he tends to be separate from others; to reduce his anxieties by helping him deal with them; to learn to accept failure and use it in a way that will lead to success; and to approach learning by way of experimentation, and experimentation without the stress of constant supervision and evaluation.

Further, you may help him by being nurturant to and supportive of his attempts to create; by allowing him to work within a set of values he had some part in setting and so obtain his commitment to what he does; by taking care of his more basic needs of body, safety, love and esteem so that he can do the things that will lead to self-fulfillment; by helping him to understand and value himself and his ideas; by encouraging him to play about with his ideas and draw from his preconscious; by praising new formed ideas and encouraging their development; and by helping him to get along with others and to overcome the difficulty of finding friends who are also gifted.

There are periods in a child's life when he is most affected by the stress and strain of growing up so that his creativity suffers. This has been found to be just at the time the child enters first grade, at the fourth grade level, entry in junior high school and high school. Not only demands put on him by the school, his peers and teachers, but also changes in school seem to affect him adversely. The worst of the slumps seems to take place at the fourth grade level, and this tends to happen when the child experiences developmental changes that bring about a shift in focus to his life, so that control of the environment through affectional relations of the parent of the opposite sex, which is central to his creativity at this time, shifts to control of the environment through increased understanding of it. At these times you can help him by reducing the tensions of change and restriction, by establishing caring relations with him, by providing stimulating creative activities and conditions of learning, and by encouraging greater use of fantasy, analogy, and the creative imagination. You may also show that you appreciate his use of creative abilities and productions, and reward him for his efforts.

You will note that there are times when your child will be more creative than others—a time at which a kind of welling up of some super energy takes place that transforms the everyday activities and happenings into something "rich and strange"; and there are other times when this dynamic play of forces do not occur. Be sensitive to these fluctuations in his life, supporting and approving of creative thoughts and deeds that do occur, and arranging for circumstances that will facilitate similar creative occurrences during the low periods. You have it in your power to cause creativity to happen and flourish before your very eyes. Be the catalyst of the mystery and magic of existence, for in the creativity of your child may lie a magnificent future for all.

References

Barron, F. *Creativity and psychological health.* Princeton, N.J.: D. Van Nostrand, 1963.

Barron, F. *Creativity and personal freedom.* Princeton, N.J.: D. Van Nostrand, 1968.

Cox, C. M. *Genetic studies of genius: Vol II, the early mental traits of three hundred geniuses.* Stanford, Calif.: Stanford University Press, 1969.

Clymer, T., and Gates, D. *May I come in?* Boston, Mass.: Ginn, 1969.

Cunnington, B. F., and Torrance, E. P. *Sounds and Images: Teacher's guide and recorded text (children's version).* Boston, Mass.: Ginn, 1965. (a)

Cunnington, B. F., and Torrance, E. P. *Imagi/Craft Series.* Boston, Mass.: Ginn, 1965. (b)

Feldhusen, J. F., and Treffinger, D. J. *Teaching creative thinking and problem solving.* Dubuque, Iowa: Kendall-Hunt, 1977.

Gordon, W. J. J. *Synectics: The development of creative capacity.* New York: Harper & Row, 1961.

Gordon, W. J. J., and Associates. *Making it strange.* Cambridge, Mass.: Synectics, 1966.

Gordon, W. J. J. On being explicit about creative process. *Journal of Creative Behavior*, 1972, 6(4), 295-300.

Gowan, J. C. The underachieving gifted child: A problem for

everyone. *Exceptional Children*, 1955, 21, 247-250.

Gowan, J. C. *Development of the creative individual.* San Diego, Calif.: Robert R. Knapp, 1971.

Gowan, J. C. *Development of the psychedelic individual.* Buffalo, N.Y.: Creative Education Foundation, 1974.

Gowan, J. C. *Trance, art and creativity.* Buffalo, N.Y.: Creative Education Foundation, 1975.

Gowan, J. C., Torrance, E. P. (Eds.) *Educating the ablest.* Itasca, Ill.: F. E. Peacock, 1971.

Guilford, J. P. *The nature of human intelligence.* New York: McGraw-Hill, 1967.

Guilford, J. P. *Creativity tests for children: A manual of interpretation.* Beverly Hills, Calif.: Sheridan Psychological Services, 1971.

Khatena, J. Children's version of Onomatopoeia and Images: A preliminary validity study of verbal originality. *Perceptual and Motor Skills*, 1971, 33, 26. (a)

Khatena, J. Something About Myself: A brief screening device for identifying creatively gifted adolescents and adults. *Gifted Child Quarterly*, 1971, 15(4), 262-266. (b)

Khatena, J. Production of original verbal images by children between the ages 8 and 19 as measures by the alternate forms of Onomatopoeia and Images. *Proceedings, 79th Annual Convention, APA*, 1971, 187-188. (c)

Khatena, J. Project talented and gifted first evaluation report. (ESEA Title III, Region II, W.Va.). Prepared for the West Virginia State Department of Education, Charleston, W.V., 1974 (Unpublished manuscript).

Khatena, J. Developmental patterns and creative orientations on Something About Myself. *Talents and Gifts*, 1975, 17(3), 23-26.

Khatena, J. Facilitating the creative functions of the gifted. *Gifted Child Quarterly*, 1977, 21(2), 218-227. (a)

Khatena, J. Creative imagination and what we can do about it. *Gifted Child Quarterly*, 1977, 21(1), 84-97. (b)

Khatena, J., and Fisher, S. A four year study of children's responses to onomatopoeic stimuli. *Perceptual and Motor Skills*, 1974, 39, 1062.

Khatena, J., and Torrance, E. P. *Thinking Creatively with Sounds and Words: Norms-technical manual* (rsch. ed.). Lexington, Mass.: Personnel Press, 1973.

Khatena, J., and Torrance, E. P. *Khatena-Torrance Creative Perception Inventory: Norms-technical manual* (rsch. ed.). Chicago, Ill.: Stoelting, 1976.

Kubie, L. W. *Neurotic distortion of the creative process.* New York: Noonday Press, 1958.

Marland, S. P., Jr. *Education of the gifted and talented (Vol. I & II): Report to the Congress of the United States.* Washington, D.C.: U.S. Government Printing Office, 1972.

Meeker, N. M., and Sexton, K. *Structure of intellect workbooks.* Los Angeles, Calif.: Loyola-Marymount Education Department, n.d.

Moreno, J. L. *Psychodrama* (Vol. I). Beacon, N.Y.: Beacon House, 1946.

Oden, M. H. *The fulfillment of promise: 40-year follow-up of the Terman gifted group.* Stanford University, California, Department of Psychology, 1968 (ERIC Document Reproduction Service No. EC 02 1968).

Open, M. B. Gifted child in a small town: A parent's point of view. *Gifted Child Quarterly*, 1970, 14(2), 92-95.

Osborn, A. F. *Your creative power.* New York: Charles Scribner's 1945.

Parnes, S. J., Noller, R. B., & Biondi, A. M. *Guide to creative action* (rev. ed. of *Creative behavior guidebook*). New York: Charles Scribner's, 1977. (a)

Parnes, S. J., Noller, R. B., & Biondi, A. M. *Creative actionbook* (rev. ed. of *Creative behavior workbook*). New York: Charles Scribner's, 1977. (b)

Pepinsky, P. Study of productive nonconformity. *Gifted Child Quarterly*, 1960, 4, 81-85.

Pippin, M. R. How does one know if a child is gifted?: Letter to the Editor. *Gifted Child Quarterly,* 1967, 11(1), 65.

Prince, G. M. The operational mechanism of Synectics. *Journal of Creative Behavior,* 1968, 2, 1-13.

Renzulli, J. S. *New Directions in creativity.* Harper & Row, 1970

Rogers, C. R. Toward a theory of creativity. *ETC: A Review of General Semantics,* 1954, 11, 249-260.

Terman, L. M. *The gifted group at mid-life: Thirty-five years' follow-up of the superior child (Genetic Studies of Genius. Vol. 5).* Stanford, Ca.: Stanford University Press, 1959.

Torrance, E. P. *Guiding creative talent.* Englewood Cliffs, N.J.: Prentice-Hall, 1962.

Torrance, E. P. Understanding the fourth grade slump in creative thinking. (Final Report on Cooperative Research Project No. 994, Office of Education), Athens, Ga.: Georgia Studies of Creative Behavior, University of Georgia, 1967 (Unpublished manuscript).

Torrance, E. P. A longitudinal exmination of the fourth grade slump in creativity. *Gifted Child Quarterly,* 1968, 12(4), 195-199. (a)

Torrance, E. P. Examples and rationales of test tasks for assessing creative abilities. *Journal of Creative Behavior,* 1968, 2, 165-178. (b)

Torrance, E. P. Can we teach children to think creatively? *Journal of Creative Behavior,* 1972, 6(2), 114-143.

Torrance, E. P. *Torrance Tests of Creative Thinking: Norms-technical manual.* Lexington, Mass.: Personnel Press, 1974.

Torrance, E. P. Sociodrama as a creative problem-solving approach to studying the future. *Journal of Creative Behavior,* 1975, 9(3), 182-195.

Torrance, E. P., Khatena, J., & Cunnington, B. F. *Thinking Creatively with Sounds and Words.* Lexington, Mass.: Personnel Press, 1973.

Wechsler, E. *The measurement and appraisal of adult intelligence.* Baltimore: Williams & Wilkins, 1966.

Williams, F. E. *Classroom ideas for encouraging thinking and feeling.* Buffalo, N.Y.: D. O. K., 1970.